Man in the Field of Responsibility

Man in the Field of Responsibility

Karol Wojtyła

Translated by
Kenneth W. Kemp
&
Zuzanna Maślanka Kieroń

Introduction by Fr. Alfred Wierzbicki

St. Augustine's Press
South Bend, Indiana

Manufactured in the United States of America

1 2 3 4 5 6 16 15 14 13 12 11

Library of Congress Cataloging in Publication Data
John Paul II, Pope, 1920–2005.
[Człowiek w polu odpowiedzialności. English]
Man in the field of responsibility / by Karol Wojtyla;
translated by Kenneth W. Kemp & Zuzanna Maslanka Kieron;
introduction by Alfred Wierzbicki.
p. cm.
Includes index.
ISBN 978-1-58731-491-9 (hardback: alk. paper)
1. Christian ethics – Catholic authors. I. Title.
BJ1249.J5613 2011
241'.042 – dc22   2011010061

St. Augustine's Press
www.staugustine.net

Table of Contents

Introduction

Fr. Alfred Marek Wierzbicki
Professor of Ethics and
Director of the John Paul II Institute
at the John Paul II Catholic University of Lublin

THE LAST PHILOSOPHICAL BOOK OF KAROL WOJTYŁA APPEARED in Polish only in 1991, when its author had already become Pope. It was immediately noticed by Italian publishers and thus has appeared in two editions, but outside of Poland and Italy, it is still little-known. One must hope that its translation into English will obtain for it new readers in broader circles of those interested in the philosophical thought of Karol Wojtyła, which serves as the intellectual background of the pontificate of John Paul II, as well as of those interested in the conception of ethics on which Wojtyła himself worked very intensively over the course of many years.

It is an unfinished book, barely the outline of a book which Karol Wojtyła intended to write in collaboration with his former student, Fr. Tadeusz Styczeń. It was precisely to him that, in 1972, he sent the seventy-four-page manuscript with a sketch of the first part of a book about the conception and the methodology of ethics. In a letter to the co-author of the planned book, he wrote, "I am sending a conspectus of the work we are supposed to write together. The conspectus is a first draft and a first attempt to put my thoughts in order. It is very uneven and written just before vacation. In any case it can serve as some kind of basis of discussion—and therefore I am sending it, counting on the possibility of discussing it with you in the second half of August."[1]

It is important to notice that this letter is a valuable testimony to the style of the academic work of Professor Karol Wojtyła, who was at that time already a cardinal. For his works were born in discussion with his students. He greatly valued academic seminars as an incomparable occasion for common reflection and the search for truth. The manuscript sent to Fr. Styczeń in fact became the foundation for several meetings and discussions between Karol Wojtyła and his co-workers in the Department of Ethics at the Catholic University of Lublin, but the intended textbook of ethics was not finished by 16 October 1978. When one of the authors of that planned book became Pope, further work by the two authors on a joint book became impossible. Happily, however, in 1991, Fr. Tadeusz Styczeń, with the agreement of John Paul II, decided to publish the unfinished ethical work of his teacher, thanks to which we have not only a vision of a new book by Wojtyła about ethics, but above all a brief outline of the point of arrival of his many years of reflection on the essence of morality and reflection on the theme of ethics as a philosophical theory of the experience of morality.

The study of ethics was not just an episode in the biography of the late Pope, for he worked on ethics systematically and with

---

1   A. Szostek cites a fragment of this letter in the introduction to the Polish edition, Karol Wojtyła, *Człowiek w polu odpowiedalności* (Instytut Jana Pawła II KUL, 1991), pp. 12–13.

great scholarly passion within the context of his duties as a lecturer and as the director of the Department of Ethics at the Catholic University of Lublin from 1954 to 1978. Lublin was at that time home to a philosophical circle which had faced the existential violence of two totalitarianisms—Nazism and Communism—which had shaken and destroyed an entire system of values hitherto recognized as absolute and inviolable. In that historical situation, the philosophers who made up that circle raised questions about the very foundations of philosophy, conscious of the need for a new formulation of traditional philosophy or even a correction of it. Karol Wojtyła introduced into that circle an exceptional sensitivity to the dignity of man as a person.

In the theoretical dimension, that sensitivity is translated into a bold attempt to develop personalism, which led eventually to the necessity of elaborating a synthesis of an objectively and realistically oriented philosophy of being, inspired by the achievements of St. Thomas Aquinas, with a modern philosophy of the subject, sometimes understood as a philosophy of consciousness. Let us cite the opinion of Fr. Tadeusz Styczeń on the originality and importance of the thought of Karol Wojtyła for the formation of the Lublin School of Philosophy, which is often too hastily presented as a version of Thomism.

I think that it was Karol Wojtyła who 'infected' the Lublin philosophical circle—and even today soundly agitates it—with his *personalism*. [...] Discovery of the duty to love one's fellow man is therefore a case of man's *experience*, a case of seeing him 'differently' and 'as something higher,' and not a *theory* of man, not just a conclusion in some kind of system or a definition of the person worked out as the result of laborious investigations.[2]

2   T. Styczeń and E. Balawajder, *Jedynie prawda wyzwala. Rozmowy o Janie Pawle II* (Roma: Polski Instytut Kultury Chrześcijańskiej, 1986), p. 26.

Karol Wojtyła as a philosopher on the one hand had deep thoughts drawn from the experience of a man and on the other hand did not have a ready philosophy, fully capable of systematizing and explaining the elementary data of experience concerning the essence of man and of the moral order. That philosophy had to be formed into a well-grounded theory which explores the richness of experience. Personalism turned out to be such a theory, discussed as it was in such a lively way in Continental philosophy in the first half of the twentieth century, especially in France and Germany. The work of Karol Wojtyła is not, however, a part of any of those trends.

No doubt the theoretical impulse to investigate the problems posed by personalism flowed from a penetrating analysis of the ethical system of Max Scheler, but indirectly, through the work of Scheler, also from an analysis of the personalist position in ethics, one initiated in a new way—against the background of the entire earlier ethical tradition—by Immanuel Kant. Karol Wojtyła, as a young philosopher at the beginning of his academic career in the 1950s, showed a fascination with the personalist thought of both Kant and Scheler and he worked out a deep critique of their concepts of the person, which, in the opinion of Wojtyła, were charged with similar errors of apriorism, despite being formulated differently by the two philosophers. From the very beginning of his philosophical reflections on the person, Wojtyła remained convinced of the necessity of developing a realistic metaphysics of the person on the basis of a philosophy of being. In that aspect of his personalism, he remained indebted to Aquinas, who saw in the person the perfection of being: *persona significat id quo est perfectissimum in tota natura, scilicet subsistens in rationali natura* ["Person" signifies what is most perfect in all nature—that is, a subsistent individual of a rational nature].[3]

Karol Wojtyła worked out the framework of ethical personalism in his work *Love and Responsibility*, a work in the area of sexual and marital ethics. Before, however, the author undertakes detailed ethical considerations on the theme of love between man and woman, he carries out a fundamental analysis of the truth about the human person, as a result of which he arrives at a normative conclusion questioning the Utilitarian approach in ethics. The dignity of the person does not allow the person to be made a means or to be used. Karol Wojtyła calls the fundamental norm of morality the personalistic norm.

This norm, in its negative aspect, states that the person is the kind of good which does not admit of use and cannot be treated as an object of use and as such the means to an end. In its positive form, the personalistic norm confirms this: the person is a good towards which the only proper and adequate attitude is love. This positive content of the personalistic norm is precisely what the commandment to love teaches.[4]

Wojtyła's critique of Utilitarianism, like Kant's, is based on presenting the person as the source of moral law. While for Kant the principle of autonomy is sufficient to ground the positive content of the categorical imperative, Wojtyła looks for the metaphysical foundations of the personalistic norm, foundations which reside in the being and goodness of the person. The personalistic norm has its rational content, understood in

3   St. Thomas Aquinas, *Summa Theologiae*, I, 29.3.
4   Towarzystwo Naukowe KUL, 1986. English translation by H.T. Willetts (Farrar, Straus, Giroux, 1981), p. 41.

light of the experience of the goodness of the person, and therefore via the existential meeting of person and person, especially in the lived experience of love. In such love is found both a fascination with a particular person and the choice of one person among many others as someone unique, as well as an attitude of responsibility of one person for another. The personalistic norm converges with the Christian precept of love.

In the domain of ethical discourse, that precept is not, however, treated as an argument in favor of the personalistic norm, but adds to that norm a rationality already perfectly clear at the level of experience. One must note how Wojtyła assigns the essential role in moral discourse to metaphysics, which puts him in opposition to the position taken on this matter by Kant. What further distinguishes him from Kant is his view on the coherence and possibility of the data of faith and reason supplementing one another. One should not, however, forget that Karol Wojtyła's formulation of the personalistic norm is, as a matter of fact, an attempt to make a metaphysical interpretation of Kant's second, or personalist, formulation of the categorical imperative. That shows that Karol Wojtyła's personalism is not so much a reception of Kant's personalism and an application of it to particular moral issues, as it is an important correction of it.

Love and Responsibility, published in 1960, contains two important elements. First, in that book Wojtyła presents the personalistic norm as the fundamental norm of morality, converging and corresponding as to its content with the Christian precept of love. Second, he applies the personalistic norm which he had worked out—in light of analyses of the essence of morality—to particular matters in the field of sexual ethics, and through it also indicates its argumentative significance. We have, therefore, already in *Love and Responsibility*, a well-developed proposal for a personalist formulation of ethics. One could expect that Wojtyła would undertake a broader attempt to apply the personalist principle as the argumentative key to a wide array of diverse moral problems. Indeed some of his students undertook that work, while Karol Wojtyła himself, in the 1960s, concentrated his attention on the problem of the person. He shifted his interest from the purely ethical to the field of the philosophy of man. In 1969 appeared *Person and Act*, the author of which provided the significant subtitle, *An Anthropological Study.*

There certainly were pastoral reasons why the Cardinal Archbishop of Cracow and Lublin professor occupied himself with the problem of the nature of the person during the years of the Second Vatican Council (1962–65) and those immediately following. Karol Wojtyła's participation in the Council, as Rocco Buttiglione emphasizes, strengthened the conviction of the then-young bishop from Poland about the central significance of the question of the person for fruitful dialogue between the Church and modernity.[5] Karol Wojtyła himself gave expression to that conviction as early as 1964:

The human person is one of the elements of the doctrine of the Second Vatican Council. Although not one of the prepared constitutions or decrees has the human person as its direct subject, that subject is nevertheless present at a very deep level throughout the teaching of the Council, teaching which has gradually been emerging in our work over the last several years. The Council expresses itself directly in its teaching. Teaching

5   Rocco Buttiglione, *Karol Wojtyla: The Thought of the Man who Became Pope John Paul II* (Eerdmans, 1997), 178–87.

is its work, and in turn that teaching has to penetrate to the consciousness of the Church and to express itself in the activity of the Church. It is necessary that the human person have its due place in the teaching of the Council, a place from which will flow its proper place in the activity of the Church; it will be a great contribution to the pastoral goals of the Council.[6]

In the case of Karol Wojtyła, it is not possible to speak about a "personalist turn" occasioned by the Council, since he belonged to those very participants of the Second Vatican Council who arrived at the Council with already well-developed personalist sensitivities. Even more, Karol Wojtyła had already gained recognition for his developing philosophical reflections centered on the theme of the human person. A consequence of his earlier attempts to apply personalist arguments in ethics turned out to be the undertaking of a line of thought in the field of the philosophy of the person that would allow him to look more closely and more insightfully at that unusual being among beings which is the person. *Person and Act* must be read from the perspective of the development of Karol Wojtyła's original personalist thought, as a deepening of the metaphysical foundation on which the ethico-normative judgments proposed in *Love and Responsibility* are based. For both books remain in an intriguing mutual relation of dependence and development, accounting by that fact for the conspicuous coherence of the philosophical thought of their author.

In Wojtyła's book about the person, the field of inquiry is precisely narrowed to viewing the person through the act. Let us note in passing, that the English translation of the title of

6   "Człowiek jest osobą" ["Man is a Person"], *Tygodnik Powszechny* (1964), no. 52, p. 2.

that book (*The Acting Person*[7]) is inaccurate, since for the author it is not a matter of a view of human action or of a view of man as an acting being, but of a metaphysical reduction of the human act to its ontic source, which is the person. What a person is is revealed in light of his act, in accordance with the classical principle *operari sequitur esse* [action follows being], to which Wojtyła refers directly, showing the presence of a metaphysical dimension in the phenomenological analysis of the experience "man acts."

That narrowing of the inquiry to viewing a person through acts brings with it, as Wojtyła says, a "factoring out" of the problem set of ethics. That does not mean that that problem set is without significance for anthropology itself. For Wojtyła it is a matter of the methodological separation of ethics from anthropology as two distinct fields of philosophical inquiry into human affairs. What is more, he thinks that such a phenomenological separation of the experience "man acts" from the experience of morality itself as an aspect of a broader and multifaceted experience of man allows one more accurately to establish the essential and necessary relations between anthropology and ethics, relations which have been abstracted and elaborated from the days of Socrates and Aristotle. Let us recall his own commentary on the proper sense of the mathematical metaphor of "factoring something out":[8]

> "Factoring something out" has as its aim the simplification of an expression; it does not have as its aim either the

7   Edited by Anna T. Tymieniecka (Reidel, 1979).

8   Wojtyła has in mind the operation which allows one to rewrite certain mathematical expressions, e.g., "(3x + 6)" as "3 (x + 2)." The term used here is the term used in Polish to translate Edmund Husserl's procedure of "bracketing."—Translators.

rejection of that which is factored out or severing the connection between that which is factored out and that which is left inside the parentheses. Quite the contrary, factoring an element out places a greater emphasis on the presence and significance of that element in the entire expression. If the element were not factored out, it would only be hidden in another element of the expression. Thanks to its removal outside the parentheses, it becomes manifest and is easily seen.

Thus similarly, the person-act problem, traditionally a problem situated within ethics, can, once ethics is factored out, reveal itself more fully, not only in its own reality, but also in that rich reality which human morality is.[9]

The above-mentioned remarks on the subject of "factoring out" the experience of morality in considerations on the topic of the person seem to foreshadow the possibility, and even to some extent simply the necessity, of writing a book and undertaking an analysis of the fact of morality in the context of a personalist formulation of ethics on the richer foundation of knowledge about man himself as a person—knowledge obtained via analysis of the person in light of experience of the human act. The work *Man in the Field of Responsibility*, which, as has already been said, was never finished by its author, grows precisely from the idea of a more complete personalist elaboration of ethics. Along with *Love and Responsibility* and *Person and Act*, this book constitutes a personalist trilogy in which is found an expression of the development of the philosophy of Karol Wojtyła. In the entirety of Wojtyła's philosophical thought, one can see two mutually complementary movements:

9   *Osoba i czyn* (Towarzystwo Naukowe KUL, 2000), 61–62. Translation ours. The passage can be found in the Tymieniecka edition on pp. 13–14.

first from ethics to anthropology and later from anthropology to ethics.

Man in the Field of Responsibility does not raise moral questions directly; it is a work on the subject of ethics itself. The author's attention is focused on the conception and methodology of ethics, and it must therefore be recognized as a work in the field of metaethics, of course in the broader sense of that term. It is easy to see that Wojtyła presents a cognitivist approach to metaethics. It is difficult, however, to find in his thought even a reflection of the debate between cognitivism and emotivism, or of the debate carried on within cognitivism itself between intuitionism and naturalism. When, however, we look at the critique of Utilitarianism conducted on the basis of personalism, we find also an important point of contact with the debate conducted within twentieth-century Anglo-Saxon philosophy. Emphasizing the methodological independence of ethics from theology, metaphysics, anthropology, and the empirical sciences, including the descriptive studies of morality (such as the sociology of morality, the psychology of morality, and the history of morality), Wojtyła shows the objective, rational, universal character of ethical discourse, rooted in the experience of morality.

The experiential point of departure for ethics required a ethics and its method which appeared in the philosophical tradition of the West. The mentality of Karol Wojtyła is generally characterized by a great intellectual kindness in the face of conceptions formulated by other authors. He associates phenomenological attention to things in themselves with an insightful study of their conceptualization and understanding by other philosophers. This leads to his own philosophical style being profoundly characterized by dialogue with positions that have been elaborated over the course of the history of ethics, and often by discussion entirely open to criticism. Wojtyła expresses the conviction that mistaken theories often arise as a result of detaching one aspect of morality and treating it as if it were the whole. Therefore, phenomenological analysis should allow for a more complete synthesis of the various formulations which grew from the absolutization of a certain aspect of morality. This is a position free of eclecticism, since the final point of reference becomes here the reality given in experience, and not exclusively ideas.

A concern for the integral formulation of aspects of that very experience of morality allows Wojtyła to treat ethics as a science that is practical and normative at the same time. In that synthesis, there is a place for the unification of the praxiological layer of the experience of morality (act), with the deontological layer (norm) and the axiological layer (good, value). In that way, in the case of the analysis of the experience of morality, Wojtyła is able to see the truth of the formulation of ethics as a practical science in the Aristotelian-Thomistic tradition, but also the truth of the formulation of ethics as a normative science by Kant and the truth of the formulation of ethics by Scheler as a science about values. On the other hand, the author of *Man in the Field of Responsibility* correctly points out the limits of each of these formulations. The interpretation of experience finally depends on the insightful disclosure of aspects of, and on an attempt to secure a comprehensive view of, some kind of reality. In the case of a matter that is as subtle, and as close to man, as is morality, concern about its adequate and possibly full formulation is greatly to be valued.

Let us return our attention once again to an element present in Wojtyła's attempt to synthesize the aspects of moral experience into the conception of ethics. Most of our ethical disputes do not in fact concern the content of moral duties themselves. Even in the face of a crisis of morality the still fundamentally human moral sensitivities remain unchanged. Most people can repeat with Kant: "the moral law within me" or, with the classical tradition, "good is to be done; evil avoided." I do not in the least claim that there are no sharp moral controversies; I am, however, expressing the view that moral consciousness is lasting and more primordial than ethical inquiry. However, a significant part of our debates seems to be disputes concerning ethical argumentation and is a matter of questioning the relevance of certain kinds of argument, as well as their soundness. Karol Wojtyła, as an ethicist, was profoundly aware of that problem. That can be seen in his immensely interesting attempt to see the relation between natural law and personalist argumentation as one of complementarity rather than as one of opposition.

That proposal, sketched only in outline in the book *Man in the Field of Responsibility*, was deepened in the papal encyclical *Veritatis Splendor* (1994), which discussed the controversy between the natural law tradition and the radical version of personalism which eliminates the category of nature from the field of ethics.

Acknowledgments

We would like to thank Sr. Theresa Sandok, O.S.M., for many helpful suggestions on points of translation and Julie Lasher for help in preparing the index.

Man in the Field of Responsibility

Introduction

THIS STUDY ON THE SUBJECT OF THE CONCEPTION AND methodology of ethics is the fruit of and a retrospective look at research conducted over many years as well as of on-going discussions among academics in Lublin. Those discussions concern the fundamental problems of ethics as a science.[1] They arise out of an old philosophical tradition, but at the same time remain in critical contact with the whole multifaceted development of the ethical problematic in contemporary philosophical thought. In addition, they seek to overcome the discordance that has found its way into this thought as a result of divergent epistemological principles.

In such a situation, one can either adopt one of the sides of the discordant picture of reality or search for a point of departure in which that discordance proves to be artificial (or at least to a certain extent artificial and imaginary). In any case, the conception of ethics offered here contains in its point of departure an attitude which is not only critical but also open. The discussion held in the philosophical circle mentioned above always had such a character. The philosophers who participated in that

---

1   Wojtyła uses this term in the traditional sense, *scientia* or *Wissenschaft*, not in the narrower sense in which the English word is sometimes used.—Translators

3

discussion not only sought for themselves "within the circle" contact with the broadest possible (and orientationally differentiated) philosophical problematic in ethics, but also constantly compared their own inquiries with the available results of the inquiries of other philosophers interested in ethics, in particular those philosophers associated with the journal *Etyka*, who generally had a Marxist orientation.

The Lublin circle attached fundamental importance to the question of *ethics as a science*, and even more to what is known as *metaethics* (Fr. Tadeusz Styczeń)—and those inquiries also find expression in this study. It has, therefore, the character of a metaethical work, but not in the particular and narrow sense found in some approaches, in which metaethics is understood as the rejection of the possibility of ethics as a science. According to the position which I intend to present in this study, metaethics means the set of cognitive steps which have as their goal the validation of ethics precisely as a science.

Having thus first explained the subtitle of this book,[2] it remains to explain the title. The book is to some extent *a continuation of the study "Person and Act."* In that work I presented a philosophical analysis of the person as a reality to which we have access in experience. The person manifests himself in and through his act. At the starting point for the entire many-faceted analysis of the human person lies the experience of the human being. That experience—as I showed in *Person and Act*—contains the experience of morality as its integral element, without which it would simply be impossible to construct a theory of the person.

2   [The manuscript of this work does not include a subtitle. The contents of the previous paragraph suggest that perhaps Wojtyła had in mind *Man in the Field of Responsibility: A Metaethical Study*; he had given his previous work the title, *Love and Responsibility: An Ethical Study*.—Translators]

At the same time, however—though relying throughout the study of the person on the experience of morality and constructing the study in a certain way primarily on the basis of that experience—I programmatically "factored morality out." That is, in my study of the person I did not subject morality itself to analysis. That is precisely what I now intend to do in this study: This will be a study of morality as such.

In mathematics one speaks of "factoring out" precisely when the element to be factored out is originally present within the parentheses. That was the case in the previous study—and that will also be true in this one. In a certain sense, I intend here to analyze that which *was factored out in the previous study: morality* as a reality subjectivized in the person. But precisely that phrase testifies to the fact that the reality of the person inheres in morality, that morality is a thoroughly specific and connatural reality with respect to the person—with respect precisely to the person and only to the person.

PART I
Morality as the Field Proper to Ethics

1. The Problem of the Experience of Morality

POSING THE PROBLEM OF "MORALITY AS THE FIELD PROPER TO ethics," I intend to speak in the first place about the experience of morality. That experience is contained within the experience of the human being and occupies in it a more or less central position. The experience of morality must be extracted from the entirety of the experience of the human being as a reality "in itself." That extraction belongs to the process of understanding. Here one should recall the fundamental principles of *Person and Act* concerning the strict connection and mutual relation of experience with understanding. [Citations needed here.][1] That which we call *the experience of morality* is at the same time from the very beginning already a kind of understanding of morality. It is because of that understanding that morality becomes the proper field of ethics. Ethics is nothing other than the process of understanding the reality which constitutes morality, brought "to completion." In order, however, to undertake and conduct that process, one must precisely define its beginning, i.e., the experience of morality.

---

1   Notes in square brackets are from the original manuscript. —Translators

7

That experience is contained in the experience of the human being, or, more precisely, in the fact: "man acts," and in its communal dimension: "man acts together with others."

The *proper element* of morality is contained in *the experience of duty,* the lived experience[2] strictly connected to every concrete subject when that subject is the cause of an act and experiences its own efficacy. The lived experience of duty ("I ought to …") is always strictly personal and connected to the concrete "I act" even when that action is performed "together with others."

The lived experience of duty is in a way contained in efficacy and the lived experience of it—and is in a way external and prior to it ("I ought to act" or "I ought not to act") when the duty determines efficacy. That duty which is already contained in efficacy, in a given action, concerns the object or the end of the action ("I ought to do x"). These two aspects of duty are not in reality distinct, but are very closely connected with one another ("I ought to act, in order to accomplish x"—"I ought not to act, in order not to accomplish y").

[A fuller picture:
    a) I ought to act, in order to realize x
    b) I ought to act, in order not to realize y

2   Wojtyła here relies on Edmund Husserl's distinction between *Erfahrung* and *Erlebnis,* a distinction difficult to render into English, as for both the ordinary English word would be *experience. Erfahrung* (Polish *doświadczenie*) refers to the objective content of a person's contact with some reality, whereas *Erlebnis* (Polish *przeżycie*) refers to the subjective dimension reflected in consciousness. In order to maintain the distinction we follow the practice of Husserl scholars in rendering the latter as *lived experience.* For more on this, see Karol Wojtyła, "Subjectivity and the Irreducible in the Human Being," in Teresa Sandok, OSM, translator, *Person and Community: Selected Essays* (Peter Lang, 1993), 209–217, especially §3.—Translators

    c) I ought not to act, in order to realize *x*

    d) I ought not to act, in order not to realize *y*

Examples would make this clearer].

In any case the experience of duty comes in two forms: positive and negative, action or inaction, the realization of a certain objective state or its non-realization.

In order to make the problem of the experience of morality more precise, one must ask oneself two more questions:

1. whether the experience of morality is identical with the lived experience of duty?
2. whether it is limited to that lived experience?

One must answer these questions both together and separately.

Together: the lived experience of duty is only a *constitutive element* of the experience of morality.

Separately:

Ad 1. The experience of morality is not identical with every lived experience of duty. Only the lived experience of moral duty can be said to be a constitutive element of the experience of morality. It is necessary, however, to recognize that in addition to the experience of duty in the moral sense, i.e., duty proper to the act and its accomplishment, there is also the lived experience of duty in the "technical" sense which is connected with production. Because production is also an action, an act of a person, duty in the "technical" sense enters into duty in the moral sense. Nevertheless, the two are not to be identified—and for that reason, too, one must say that the lived experience of duty is not in every sense a constitutive element of moral experience.

Ad 2. Although the lived experience of duty in the moral

sense is a constitutive element of the experience of morality, that experience *is not limited only to that element.* We are inclined to take for the experience of morality in the broader (and also everyday) sense an entire cluster of facts which manifest moral good and evil. Those facts are strictly connected with human action (both "I act" and "I act together with others") and possess a personal (inner-personal) as well as an interpersonal and social dimension. Among the facts which we include in the experience of morality are moral good and evil as a consequence of actions, a personal consequence or a social consequence (e.g., when we speak of the moral corruption or moral loftiness of an individual or society).

One can say that the experience of morality possesses, as it were, different layers and different aspects. The layer to which the experience of morality at first points, in a way, is moral good or evil as a certain state of the person or society (this is in a way, therefore, the *axiological* layer). At the same time that very "moral good or evil" always manifests itself in acts, is connected with them, and is their characteristic fruit (this is thus, as it were, the *praxiological* layer of the experience of morality). Nevertheless, while including both of these layers in the experience, we must always arrive ultimately at the element of moral duty as the element which constitutes every moral fact, both when we conceive human action in its purely personal dimension ("a man acts") and in its communal dimension ("a man acts together with other people"). One can define that layer of the experience of morality as the *deontological* layer.

What still must be said about the experience of morality as the foundation of ethics as a science? One must affirm that it is a foundation that is, before all else, "given," and not "imposed." That means that the experience of morality must be accepted;

it cannot be created. At the basis of ethics as a science, *experimentation*—in the sense in which it exists at the basis of other sciences—is *excluded*. [More work may be needed on this topic.]

2. Experience and Understanding

[It is necessary here at the start to discuss, at least briefly, the epistemological situation.]

After having outlined the problematic of the experience of morality, we should turn to the problem of understanding it. Because human experience is always already a kind of understanding of that which is experienced, the very outlining of the problems connected with the experience of morality (sketched above) is based on some kind of understanding of it. Still, I intend to develop a deeper and more systematic understanding of morality, beginning with the element of moral duty and its constitutive element.

However, before I undertake that task, I must, at least briefly, present *the situation in the field of epistemology.* The situation which has developed in philosophy and contemporary science has caused ethics to be—perhaps even more than other disciplines—in a state of division. One may add that that critical (i.e., "resulting from critique" in the Kantian sense) epistemological situation seems above all to concern the mutual relation of experience and understanding.

One could present that situation (which is actually far more complex) either as a divergence or as a convergence of two opposite poles: empiricism (phenomenalism, sensualism) and rationalism (apriorism). [The matter deserves broader discussion.]

Taking a closer look, one sees that these two opposing epistemological tendencies mutually condition one another and to some extent mutually trigger one another—the phenomenalism of David Hume historically set the stage for the rationalism of Immanuel Kant (apriorism)—one can say that Hume "triggered" it, although that form of rationalism is also an indirect confirmation of empiricism understood phenomenalistically and sensualistically.

On the basis of those opposing epistemological tendencies the experience of morality was made as if "impossible"—not in the sense that the same moral facts as always (especially the fact of duty) ceased to exist, but in the sense that *the proper relation between morality and understanding* was destabilized (in one way on the basis of phenomenalism, in another way on the basis of apriorism). In the context of such a rift, ethics becomes impossible, and remains only either a descriptive "science about morality" (psychology, sociology, etc.) or a particular "science of morality" (a deductive logic of norms). The fundamental understanding of morality, however, on which ethics has always depended and on which alone it can depend, is discarded.

The question whether such an understanding is possible is fundamentally a question about the experience of morality. If that question is answered affirmatively, then the answer depends on a more general *conviction about the correctness of a realist position in cognition*, in philosophy and in science. [A brief explanation of the conviction by virtue of which we accept that realist position is necessary.]

It must also be noted that we can see in contemporary thought a departure from positivistic phenomenalism, on the one hand, and from rationalism, on the other. One expression of that, among others, is the so-called phenomenological experience: a return to the fundamental unity of understanding and experience in human cognition.

3. From a Pre-scientific to a Philosophical Understanding

There is a pre-scientific understanding of morality. It is common and at the same time vague, lacking distinct conceptual or terminological contours and yet characterized by a distinct realist conviction. *Morality* is a kind of "reality." It is not merely something thought up, some kind of "idea," some kind of "*a priori*"—but it is *something real in man and among men*, in society and among societies. From that direction, a kind of inductive thread is inserted into our thinking about morality, into the understanding of it, a thread which is followed above all by the positivistic "sciences about morality": sociology, psychology, ethnology, etc. All of them apprehend morality phenomenalistically (as a phenomenon) and descriptively. However, they do not make the plane of this description of morality the very essence of morality, which they rather regard as inaccessible. On the other hand, on the plane proper to psychology or sociology they take the phenomenon of morality into account, reducing that phenomenon (in a usually informal, or even unconscious, way) to an aggregate of psychological or sociological phenomena. In that way there occurs a certain *heterogenization* of morality, its "*reductio in aliud genus* [reduction to another genus]."

That which we have from the start been calling ethics has as a point of departure above all else the "*reductio in proprium genus* [reduction to its own genus]," i.e., an understanding of the very essence of morality—and also a corresponding expression of that understanding.

Is the "inductive thread" without significance for the reductive process mentioned above? Not at all. Reduction is, above all, in itself "induction" in the Aristotelian sense. The apprehension of an essence—in this case the essence of morality—does not detach us from the entire experiential, conceptual, descriptive, or even statistical richness. Therefore, all descriptive studies "about morality" have significance for ethics. In a certain sense, ethics can even be identified with them, although it always transcends them—and does so in its very point of departure. This transcendence consists in grasping the whole of the experience of "morality as such," in an understanding of the very essence of morality.

To that understanding corresponds most closely *the kind of questions* which are posed *in connection with the experience of morality*. Those questions open the way to understanding, but in such a way that the understanding is in the questions from the beginning, that they result from it, and that they at the same time open up a further perspective of understanding. They point to what that understanding gradually and finally is about, to what man must somehow understand if his intellectual anxiety and his need to know the truth in this realm is to be satisfied. Those questions do not, therefore, possess an *a priori* character, though at the same time they go beyond the purely descriptive relation to the reality of "morality" given in experience—a relation at which the positivistically understood sciences about morality basically stop.

What kind of questions are they? One can say that they are somehow situated on the borders of the theoretical question, "*What is morality?*", in which is expressed the widely recognized need to understand that which is given in experience precisely as "morality." However, morality as an experiential fact is always given in such a way that its understanding can come about only through an understanding of those elements which constitute it in experience, i.e., in human lived experience. As has been said before, that element is, more than anything, moral duty, "*that I ought to do x.*"

From that lived experience the way of understanding leads towards the subject, towards a personal "I"—and that is the way I tried to take in *Person and Act*. From that very lived experience arises at the same time the way of an objective understanding of duty as the *constitutivum* of morality: "*what* exactly *ought I to do?*" and "*why ought I to do* what I ought to do?" Thus are formed those questions which inhere in the experience of morality as in the singularly personal "fact" (in the fact "I act"—"man acts"), and also "I act (man acts) together with others"—and which at the same time pave the way for understanding. This is an understanding of duty not only as a lived *experience*, but at the same time as an objective *fact*. That fact occurs always in relation to something—and precisely because of that "something" which I ought to do, there arises the question "why?" i.e., there arises the need to justify that fact.

The questions raised above, connected in some way with the individual fact of moral duty, can be replaced by two other questions, namely: "what is good and what is evil—and why?" In distinction from the previous questions, those last two questions have a general character. In them, we do not ask, as we did previously, about any particular duty ("what ought I to do—and why?"), but we ask about any duty and about every possible object of duty, and that not in relation to any actual duty we may have at the moment but about the object itself, about moral "good" and "evil." It seems that these questions mutually imply each other. The question: "what ought I to do and why?" is a singular case, which is similarly contained in the general question: "what is (morally) good—and why?"

Besides that, the very question—"what ought I to do and

why?"—bursts the confines of any descriptive science "about morality" and postulates from the beginning the different, non-descriptive profile of a science connected with the experience of morality. But this is already another question.

4. Understanding and Interpretation

If the questions mentioned above lead us further on the way to an understanding of morality, at the same time they point to a kind of initial understanding which lies at the foundation of any further understanding—and in fact at the foundation of the very questions which lead to that further understanding. Therefore, the entire interpretation of morality as of a reality given in experience must originate from that initial understanding and concentrate above all on it.

The initial understanding of morality as a reality given in experience is an understanding of duty, as I already asserted above. Duty itself is given in internal experience and becomes evident as a distinct fact-phenomenon, as a fact "in the person" (and at the same time a fact which is constitutive of the person).

That fact possesses a structure of its own, which cannot be separated from precisely that kind of subject: "the person." There is no way to abstract it and to consider it as a separate content (as occurs, for example, in purely semantic discussions on the topic of the relation between "is" and "ought"). The understanding of duty is the same as *determining its true significance*, and that significance cannot be determined outside the real bonds which link duty with the subject—with the person.

And it is just here that one sees confirmation of the correctness of the fundamental ethical intuition of St. Thomas. Duty always arises in strict connection with the deeper, ontic reality of the person: "*to be good or evil.*" Man "is good or evil" through his acts—he is, or rather "becomes" such because the act itself not so much "is" as each time "becomes." Duty—not as an abstraction but as a reality—always enters into just that dynamic structure. It is the spiritual structure of personal being itself [cf. *Person and Act*], on which the entire transcendence of the person in act is primarily based. That structure is at the same time reflected in consciousness and constitutes a distinct lived experience. Taking all that into account, we find that moral duty is dynamically connected with moral good and evil—and that this connection is both strict and exclusive. *Duty* arises "because of" good or evil: it is always a *specific actualization of the spiritual potentiality of a person in act*; that actualization comes out "for" good and "against" evil.

Such an understanding of duty as a key element in the entire reality that is morality allows us, in what lies ahead, to affirm the correctness of the fundamental ethical intuition of St. Thomas on the topic of *moralitas*, or, as we would say today, on the topic of moral values. According to St. Thomas *moralitas* is a genus, and "good and evil" are the two species of that genus.

The essence of "moralitas" lies in the fact that *a man, as a man, becomes good or evil through the act.* This is, therefore, a reality that is thoroughly anthropological and personalistic. It is, at the same time, axiological.

All that points to certain requirements which we encounter in undertaking an interpretation of that reality which is morality. Above all, that interpretation sets clear *ontological requirements*. In order to achieve a cognitive objectification of morality, we have to arrive at the categories of "good and evil" as properties of the very being: "man." Without that, there is no way fully to understand moral duty. It is, of course, possible to limit oneself to duty as a pure phenomenon. Since, however—in accordance with the principles of phenomenology—we are trying to reveal the entire content of that which is given in the fact (in the lived experience) of duty, *moralitas* must appear as St. Thomas understood it. [N.B. An analysis comparing St. Thomas and Max Scheler would be very interesting here.] For that reason, too, moral duty itself also ultimately requires an ontological interpretation, since the proper duty of a man is to be good "as a man."

It seems, therefore, that only on an ontological (anthropological) ground thus understood can the interpretation of morality as a reality given in experience also have an *axiological* character. For it is about good or evil—and those are values.

5. The Debate about the Interpretation of Morality

Sketching in a positive way the essential structure of that understanding which in a homogenous way corresponds to the experience of morality, we cannot however lose sight of the complexity of this matter. I mentioned earlier that, according to positivist principles, the understanding of morality as such is impossible. From that proceeds the positivist replacement of ethics with the particular sciences of morality—like psychology or sociology. At the foundation of that tendency is—as was stated above—a "*reductio in aliud genus*," i.e., a fundamental lack of understanding of morality as such. We can add that such a position has many adherents.

If however, we regard even that problem as overcome, i.e., if we accept that the understanding of morality as such (a homogenous understanding) is possible, then we are still faced with the debate over the proper interpretation of morality, one which has lasted as long as the history of philosophy. Despite the fact that this debate has lasted so long, the poles of tension clearly appeared only in the context of contemporary thought. At issue here is the understanding of morality as it is found in the various conceptions of ethics, for each of those conceptions of ethics contains within itself a kind of elementary understanding of morality and a kind of interpretation of it. *That interpretation depends* to a great extent *on one's overall conception of philosophy*, on one's gnosiological, epistemological, principles, which, as is known, fundamentally condition the relation to metaphysics. In that way also, differences in the interpretation of morality over the course of the history of philosophy (e.g., the differences in the interpretations of Plato or Aristotle, St. Thomas Aquinas or Duns Scotus, Kant or Scheler) are basically explained. We can add that one's interpretation of morality (and consequently of ethics) is not only conditioned by one's overall framework of philosophical thought, but also in turn conditions it.

However, leaving aside (to the extent possible) this system of mutually conditioning conceptions, we are trying to arrive at that *which is precisely proper to the understanding of morality itself,* that which somehow proceeds immediately from experience. What can we say about that?

It seems that it is possible to observe here (speaking most generally) the following two divergences, which somehow indicate the range of the debate on the interpretation of morality:

1. In the field of metaphysical reduction, we ultimately arrive at *man as a being* that is—and becomes—good or evil, whereas in the field of phenomenological reduction we stop at the lived experience of the particular values "good–evil": Scheler shows

how "personal being" (*personales Sein*) stands out in that lived experience, which subjectively possesses a particular depth. In that way we are witnesses to the convergence of the two interpretations and of their complementarity—although the fundamental debate remains: the debate over whether the interpretation of morality should be carried out *through being* or *through values*.

2. Another theme in the debate over the interpretation of morality is the problem of the possibility or impossibility of connecting *moral duty* (and thereby good and evil as moral values) with *teleology*. That problem belongs in fact primarily to the next part of this study, to the question of norms, but it has some relevance even here. One must add that the problem owes its origin to the position of Kant, who, in his own way, excluded teleology from morality.

Acknowledging this twofold terrain of the debate about the interpretation of morality, we must however emphasize that that debate takes place *on the basis of an understanding of morality that is fundamentally shared by* the representatives of the divergent interpretive tendencies: on the basis of the conviction that morality itself can be both understood and interpreted. Such a conviction—despite the great variety of epistemological and methodological premises—is however somehow shared by Aristotle and Kant, as well as by St. Thomas and the phenomenologists. *Beyond the limits* of that community we are faced with a decision between only two alternatives—*the positivist mentality and the neo-positivist one*, as has already been said.

Because we find that there is—within the limits of the debate about the interpretation of morality—a common conviction that morality as such can be understood and interpreted, it seems that we can "use the debate" (just as already was done in *Person and Act*) in that interpretation and for its enrichment. In that way, the interpretation of morality as a reality given in experience will consist in uncovering the aspects in which that reality appears. For morality is not a static reality, but a dynamic one.

6. The Interpretation of Morality as the Uncovering of Its Aspects

There can be no doubt that the fact of "being good or evil" (I—a man—am good or evil), or rather more the fact of "becoming good or evil as a man," is fundamental to morality. Moral duty is organically woven into that very fact. At the same time, however, there can also be no doubt that this fact which is essential to morality, and into which duty is organically woven, is given to us in lived experience. The experience of morality can be identified with the lived experience that I am— or rather that I become—good or evil. Duty is contained in that lived experience: the duty of being and of becoming good—the duty of not-being and of not-becoming evil. Since duty is a constitutive element of that lived experience, then the *experience of morality can be identified* (as we are doing here) *with the lived experience of moral duty.*

1. That state of affairs already indicates the necessity of understanding the interpretation of morality as the uncovering of its aspects. The metaphysical aspect is present in the entire experience of morality, which is an experience of being and becoming good or evil through one or another act. Becoming (*fieri*), which is a strictly metaphysical category, is contained above all in the

very experience of acting. However, it is only a substrate of the proper experience of morality, i.e., the experience of becoming morally good or evil through action: the subject itself, the "I"– the person, becomes morally good or evil. The person becomes morally good or evil through an act which is morally good or evil. Both "*becoming*" and "*being*" are *metaphysical categories* which define and express being—in this case, man as a being: as one which is, which becomes, and which becomes in and through action.

By *metaphysical reduction* in the interpretation of morality is understood the uncovering of precisely that aspect which is fundamental. Without it, one cannot speak of an understanding of morality as such, for even duty itself is insufficient for that.

At the same time it seems that in the interpretation of morality one must avoid metaphysical reduction in the radical sense, i.e., the reduction of the data of experience to the plane of being as being. For essential to the interpretation of morality is the reduction to the plane of man as being, as one which "is" in a unique way and "becomes" in a unique way. [One may add that some systems of metaphysical ethics to a certain extent have gone beyond the proper boundaries of reduction, and this must inevitably lead to the obliteration of all the distinctive features of morality as a reality given in the experience of the human being.]

2. The proper execution of metaphysical reduction, i.e., the proper uncovering of the aspect of "being and becoming good or evil as a man," allows an interpretation of morality simultaneously to uncover *the aspect of the lived experience of duty*, which—as was mentioned before—is organically rooted in the whole reality of being and becoming good or evil through

action. This is not a matter of objectivized duty, but of the lived experience of duty as a distinct subjective fact. That fact not only is given in consciousness but, as a subjective fact, is conditioned by consciousness. [Relating this to *Person and Act*, one could say that duty is given in a reflecting consciousness as a subjective fact conditioned by consciousness in its reflexive function.] Duty, while having this subjective constitution, is at the same time a fact that has objective value. It is, therefore, a certain being strictly corresponding to man, to the being of man—corresponding to being and becoming good or evil as a man. Duty is always "for" one thing and "against" another ("for" good and "against" evil).

3. A parallel uncovering of both of these aspects in the interpretation of morality allows us *to interpret morality* much more precisely *as a unique axiological reality.* That morality is such a reality has been known from the beginning: the entire interpretation is concentrated on "good and evil" as (according to St. Thomas) two species in the genus "*moralitas.*" Both the genus and the species are axiological categories. Since, however, "to be morally good" is the same as "to be good as a man," and "to be morally evil" is the same as "to be evil as a man"—morality then contains a peculiar union of axiology and ontology. This seems to be especially important with reference to the whole of phenomenology, at the basis of which value "manifests itself" above all as the content of consciousness, of lived experience, given in an intentional act with an emotive intensity all its own.

Without a doubt, *the moral values "good" and "evil" are secondarily also a content of consciousness*, a content given in an act of great emotional color. However, that is only a secondary manifestation of moral values. Scheler himself acknowledges this when he writes that moral value manifests itself "*auf dem Rücken*," somehow at the margin of action. Precisely in this secondary position, moral value is already a content that is merely known and cognitively experienced.

The primary element of the moral values "good" or "evil" *is not* however "*theoria*" *but* "*praxis.*" It is there that moral values are an actual reality: in the act, in the activity of a person, in which a man becomes good or evil. The ontological aspect of axiology is more fundamental than the gnosiological aspect. The interpretation of morality must uncover afresh both of those aspects and in proper proportion. The experience of morality shows that the cognition of the moral values "good" or "evil," in one sense, *precedes the* realization of them in action. In another sense, the cognition *follows* that realization. Both types of cognition of moral value are a *function of conscience*, in which the consciousness (or lived experience) of duty is ultimately concretized. However, conscience is more than the lived experience of duty, which pertains only to the moral value prescribed by conscience before a person acts. The judgment of conscience about moral value following the act, together with the consciousness and cognitive lived experience of good or evil (guilt) connected with that judgment, arises only after the element of duty—arises "after" the fulfillment or non-fulfillment of it.

4. The element of fulfilled or unfulfilled duty has an essential significance for the person as the subject and author of action. In the case of the fulfillment of duty, the person experiences *not only the fulfillment* of the act, but *also experiences* in that act "*the fulfillment of the self*" [cf. *Person and Act*]. In the contrary case, even despite the fulfillment of the act—or rather because of its fulfillment—the person experiences instead non-fulfillment,

disappointment in himself, and even more: guilt and sin. That entire process has an experiential, conscious character, but it reaches to the ontic structure of the person. Above all, the moral values "good–evil," as categories of being and becoming good or evil as a man, are confirmed in it. And because of that it is difficult to exclude from the interpretation of morality—as a reality given in experience—the teleological aspect. That exclusion was the work of Kant—in his case, however, it concerns above all the normative dimension of ethics (the categorical imperative, as opposed to the hypothetical, teleological imperative). Nevertheless, phenomenologists (Scheler, among others) are already beginning to see once again the teleological element, above all in human activity itself, in acts in which there is a striving for "something."

That striving alone does not yet determine the ethical profile of an act. Only moral duty does that. Moral duty, however, does not take away the dynamism of striving from a person's actions; it only directs it. That direction arises from the fact that duty brings to the striving found in human actions its own striving—the striving "for good" and "against evil." One cannot, however, agree with the view that moral values are realized somehow "alongside" other strivings (*auf dem Rücken*), although they are not themselves objects of pursuit—objects of the person's will.

The confirmation of the view that moral duty brings to a person's actions its own dynamism of striving seems to be just that special experience of fulfillment or non-fulfillment of the self (the person) which is connected (substantially, organically) with the fulfillment or non-fulfillment of moral duty. The person as a subject strives for fulfillment of himself and it is primarily in that direction that the persons's efficacy, causal power, or will is oriented. [Cf. the analyses of self-determination in *Person and Act*.] Also on that basis *"moralitas," moral value—good and evil—inscribes itself in the fundamental teleology (auto-teleology) of the person and at the same time somehow inscribes that teleology in itself.*

There remains, of course, the subtle problem of the reduction of morality to teleology—a problem which has given rise to controversy in the history of ethics, and especially in contemporary ethics. We can even agree with the view that morality (and moral value) is not reducible to a teleology of man—that morality transcends that teleology. We cannot, however, in the interpretation of morality, completely ignore the teleological aspect (auto-teleology), because in doing so we would condemn ethics to stasis and deprive it of all the dynamism proper to man as a person.

PART II

The Normativity of Ethics and the Responsibility of the Person

1. The Understanding of Morality and the Questions of Ethics.

AFTER HAVING SKETCHED IN PART I A PROBLEM WHICH SEEMS to be fundamental for the conception and methodology of ethics, it would be appropriate now, at the beginning of Part II, to take note of the fact that the problem of the experience, understanding, and interpretation of morality is by no means contained within those confines. The interpretation of morality as a fact (given in our varied experience) does not exhaust the range of questions which must be posed from the outset in connection with our experience of morality. We have already spoken about the character of those questions, about their content and their relation to experience. It is in any case worth remembering that the question which motivated the process of the understanding of morality is not so much a theoretical question about morality (what is morality? what constitutes its essence? etc.), but a question connected with concrete moral duty: what exactly ought I to do and why? as well as a generalized version of that same question: what is morally good and what is evil—and why?

The mutual relation of these questions is worthy of special attention. The question of the content (the object) of moral duty has decided priority in experience, in the existential order. This is a *question of a living morality,* which indicates both the necessity and the direction of the search for answers and explanations. Such questions (what ought I to do and why? what is good and evil and why?) are continually posed by human beings as the authors of acts, as the bearers of subjective (and objective) responsibility for each of them. In contrast, the purely theoretical question about morality is of great importance only for the various kinds of moral theorists. To what degree is that question and the answer to it important for the conception of ethics that I tried to explain previously? In order to answer questions about the object of moral duty correctly, one must already have some kind of understanding of the essence of morality, some kind of theory of it, so to speak. That does not, however, mean that the further, or especially the final, orientation of the understanding and interpretation of morality as a reality given in experience is supposed to be or could be purely theoretical. The questions which we have called here questions of ethics themselves point in that direction. Every neglect of such questions—the view that they do not belong in the realm of science—ends up relegating a science conducted on the basis of a rich and multi-faceted reality, such as morality is, to the margins of the genuine requirements of human life and existence. *De facto* the same must be said about the so-called science of morality, which does not programmatically raise the questions of ethics: what ought I to do? what is good and what is evil in human acts and why?

That is a science with positivist principles, one which excludes the possibility of obtaining a scientific answer to the above questions, seeing only the possibility of stating what—in given conditions—seems or seemed to be morally good or evil.

Meanwhile the questions which I characterized as the proper questions of ethics take us beyond those statements and require another type of answer. Precisely those questions also *give to ethics a normative character*; they instruct us first of all, in the process of understanding morality, *to recognize the "norm" as a reality entirely specific to morality*, and, in turn, to make the norm a central element of ethics as a science. Why must we do that? Precisely because it is in the moral norm (in morality) that we find the basic foundation for answers to the questions: what ought I to do and why? what is morally good and what is evil and why? Generally speaking, that is *morally good which is in accord with the norm of morality, and that is morally evil which contradicts it*, which opposes it.

Thus—and here I differ from the position of some phenomenologists (Scheler, among others)—no ascertainment of good or evil, no ascertainment of moral value, is possible without reference to the normative order, without entering into this order. This view is supported both by the experience of morality and by the fact that the central element of that experience is precisely duty—*and duty always presents some kind of norm*. The moral value of the act and of the author of the act always "appears" in that dynamic ensemble as the result of agreement or disagreement with the norm presented by duty. The norm is the essential content of duty; it also determines duty's structure and originality.

2. The World of Norms—Their Analogical Character

In connection with that, it is possible to say that, entering the world of the various duties that occur in human life and experience, we enter also into a world of norms. It is also possible to accept that that world of norms is identical to the set of contents which we can somehow abstract from these duties and consider in turn *as a category of sentences of similar character.* The category is that of *imperative sentences*—commands and prohibitions of various intensities and hues. (Thus, for example, alongside commands can be found recommendations, or even advice; alongside prohibitions, warnings, dissuasions, etc.)

Nevertheless, that whole procedure, based on an abstraction of those contents, the normative sentences, is possible and is *de facto* a broad field of logical inquiry. At the same time, however, it seems that this process of abstraction or separation from the integral reality that concrete duty always is does not yet contain the full reality of the norm, and even the most insightful inquiries of a pure philosophy of language can miss that reality. Therefore it seems that normative sentences (or formulations) must always be taken in the integral context of duty—and only in that context can they be subjected to a comparative and substantive analysis.

A comparative analysis is needed here because *the facts of duty, along with the world of norms* contained in them, *possess an analogical character* which the logical analysis of normative sentences alone might not reveal. In contrast, the goal of a comparative and substantive analysis is to reach the moral norm in its proper specificity. Such a norm is contained only in moral duty and at the same time determines its proper specificity, i.e., determines that the given duty is a moral duty. We would not be able to conduct a comparative analysis using the inductive

30

method in the positivist sense, but induction in the Aristotelian sense certainly has a place here.

1. Reflecting on norms in general (i.e., on the content of duty) in all their multiplicity, Aristotle noticed that *norms about producing something* have one kind of significance and norms about the activity or action of a person have another. Some norms have as their object the good of the work; others, the good of the agent. A different form of duty corresponds to norms of the former and latter type. Only about the latter can one say directly that it is a moral duty—about the former one can say that only indirectly: to the extent, for example, that "to be a good craftsman, or a specialist in a given field, means at the same time "to be a good man" in that field and in that respect, but it does not mean "to be good as a man" per se. Hence, technical norms (in the sense of principles of technical skill) are different from ethical norms, although there is a certain relation between them.

2. From another point of view we can distinguish, in the whole vast world of norms which combine to direct human activity, those norms which can be characterized as *norms of adaptation* to the various conditions in which man happens to perform his actions. It seems that those conditions are—speaking generally—of two kinds: psychological and sociological (whence also the development of the psychology and sociology of morality). In the case of the norms of adaptation to psychological conditions, one can list various principles of behavior (prescriptions, rules of *savoir vivre*, etc.). [Cf. on that topic the comparative analysis of "behavior" and "conduct" presented in *Person and Act*.] In the case of the norms of adaptation to sociological conditions, one can list the various canons of custom or mores, of social tradition, and even of so-called fashion.

That entire vast realm of norms and of their establishment is not directly and fundamentally identical with the sphere of morality, although it has a certain relation to ethical norms. That relation is, however, different than in the case of the technical norms distinguished above, and perhaps more complicated. From a certain point of view the norms of adaptation enter into the sphere of moral (ethical) norms and are a concretization of them (e.g., the norms of social politeness are a kind of concretization of the general norm of common life with others or even of the love of neighbor, norms concerning how to dress enter into the moral sphere, norms having to do with custom are covered by the superior norms of social morality, etc.). At the same time, however, the entire genus of norms of adaptation has, as its proper and direct object, not so much "to be good as a man" as "to present oneself well to others" against the background of the various conditions of a particular psychology or a particular sociology (social environment, nation, or social class). The latter object by no means need exclude the first and also by no means need be excluded by it—however, it is a different object: a different obligatory content and a different duty. Therefore, there is a clear basis for the distinction. N.B. This may be the basis for the "heterogenization" of the so-called sociology and psychology of morality: by not beginning from a clearly defined essence of morality, they may take to be moral norms also the various norms of adaptation.

3. Finally we come to that distinct group of norms which has such great significance for human life, especially social life, the so-called *legal norms*. They are all the more distinctive in that they usually get their formal expression or articulation from some competent authority, besides which they are enforced by

means of the administrative and punitive measures which are at the disposal of the authorities. The characteristic feature of legal norms is that they serve the so-called public order, which cannot be directly identified with the *bonum commune* (the common good) of society, although the public order should strive toward such an identity.

The relation of legal norms to moral norms—more broadly, of law to morality—has a long history in philosophic thought. It would be difficult to review that entire problematic here. One can mention that one aspect of the problem was developed by, e.g., St. Thomas, for whom law is an element of the moral order, which, in turn, has a distinct foundation in the entire order of being, while another aspect was developed, e.g., by Kant in his *distinction between morality and legality*, which to some extent opposes the one to the other. It would be difficult to follow Kant completely in this, but it seems that the correction which he introduced into the history of the problem—of course after taking account of the differences in assumptions—must not be overlooked.

Just as it is right and necessary for the public order protected by law to strive toward identity with the common good as the fundamental element of social morality, so too is it right for *law to be fundamentally connected with morality.* Nevertheless those two realities differ from one another—and there is in the world of norms and duties a foundation for distinguishing them. A legal norm is always a norm that comes "from without" and has its basis in the authority and power of government. In addition, a concern for the social good (taken maximally), and above all for public order, lies at the very nature of these norms.

That concern is not directly and immediately identifiable with the object proper to morality, "to be good as a man," although there is a mutual relation, and even a mutual inter-penetration of these aspects, just as the postulate of the maximal identification of the order of law and the order of morality must remain the general postulate of ethics and legislation.

That state of affairs, however, in no way conceals but rather reveals the fundamental non-identity of those two kinds of norms and of their establishment, and, as a consequence, of duty. Legal norms never exhaust the full range of moral norms, for law simply does not reach all the various spheres of the life and activity of the human person—above all not the internal sphere—which are subject to morality.

All that is sufficient to state that *the world of norms*, in the midst of which all human *agere* [action] takes shape, *has an analogical character*. The character of duties corresponding to those norms is analogical as well. That discovery can lead us to a closer determination of the ethical norm.

3. An Attempt at a Closer Determination of the Moral Norm

First of all, a certain clarification about terms. I use interchangeably here the expressions "the ethical norm," "the moral norm," and "the norm of morality." Each of those expressions has its justification. To some extent, the most proper seems to be the expression "the *norm of morality*," for by means of it we point to that principle of action—the act of a person—which immediately and "from within" gives that act its moral character, causing the person performing that act to become through it morally good or evil. And further, the expression "the norm of morality" points to its specific element, a kind of threshold within the dynamic connection of person and act, from which that connection enters into the dimension of morality, the ethical dimension. Before that threshold, it remains only in the ontic dimension. Of course, that very connection between person and act, even in the ontic dimension, has ethical potential. The norm of morality is the principle of actualization of that very potential.

Hence, with respect to the closer determination of the norm of morality, we cannot make that determination in the abstract, but we must make it in connection with that very potential which is proper to the person–man as simultaneously an "individual" and a "social" subject. From that norm, the entire dynamic relation to ethical norms, the readiness to conform our activity to them, gets its start. Consequently, when and only when we have before our eyes a full picture of the man–person can we understand the fact of the norm of morality, its existence and essence. We have already considered the tendency proper to the subject to fulfill itself in an act. That fulfillment of the self in an act remains closely connected with the entire dynamic structure of self-possession and self-dominion [cf. *Person and Act*], and that is also why it appears in every genuine act of self-determination. The entire structure of the person, which actualizes itself in self-determination, is ready to accept the norm of morality and conform itself to it since *the so-called suitable good (bonum honestum) corresponds to them "by nature."* Here again we appeal to the thought of St. Thomas Aquinas and of the philosophical tradition of which he is the patron. In more contemporary language, one speaks not so much about "suitability" [*godziwość*] as about the "dignity" [*godność*] of man as a person.

In Polish the root of both words is the same. All of morality (*moralitas*) as a result of the norm and of its establishment has a prior foundation in the connatural striving of the man–person toward suitability, toward dignity. Here lies its first source, not yet very precisely defined—the norm of morality allows a more precise determination and actualization of the dignity of the person.

Of course, such a state of affairs immediately reveals the norm to us as an external reality, transcendent in relation to the pursuit of suitability, which is natural to the person—but also as the reality most closely conditioned by that internal pursuit.

One could in still other terms, or also from a different, more empirical, perspective, speak here about the fundamental sensitivity to moral values as the values which most essentially allow the pursuit of the dignity of the person to be brought to proper fulfillment in man. One cannot deny that the entire immanent framework of the transcendent profile of morality carries in itself the clear mark of teleology—just that teleology which corresponds to the whole structure of self-fulfillment in the act, of which we already spoke.

As for the *axiological qualification* of "suitability" and "dignity," it seems to be as diverse as the whole philosophical foundation on which it developed. The "*bonum honestum*" of St. Thomas, like "*bonum*" in general, is identified with an end. The "dignity" of man as a person means above all a property or fundamental quality—and in this sense the "value" of the person as such: a value which belongs to man because he is a person and for which, therefore, man ought to strive.

Without regard, however, to those differences or semantic nuances, the pursuit of the dignity (suitability) proper to man as a person is a powerful and fundamental dynamism. The whole intensity of the lived experience of good and evil—especially that evil which manifests itself in the entire experience of guilt, in the pangs of conscience, etc.—testifies to the power of that dynamism. Artists and writers have done much to describe that experience, and phenomenologists (e.g., Scheler) have done much to cognitively objectify it. That has been discussed before.

It must be added here that thus and only thus can one explain the specific character of a norm which is not only *imperative*, but also *categorical*. [Cf. the conception of Kant.] According to Kant, that character shows that the norm of morality must be excluded from the teleological order altogether, since to it can correspond only hypothetical norms. It seems, however, that such a view is not convincing. The categorical character of the ethical norm shows only the particular unconditionality of moral values—it shows that they are values that must be realized, toward which *one must strive* (i.e., an end) at all costs, regardless of other values which might appear as competing ends.

Hence, the norm of morality show a *disinterested character*—and the whole Kantian conception of a categorical imperative seems above all to point to that disinterested character. That particular unconditionality of moral value and its disinterestedness is reflected in the norm of morality. Such a definition of moral value and the norm of morality causes us to look at the suitability or dignity of the person in the proper way. Someone might say that there is no true disinterestedness in morality or in the norm of morality since man in his act strives for the realization of his own dignity. It seems that here one can apply the penetrating analysis of Scheler, according to which moral values themselves are not an object of an act of will or pursuit, but are realized "on the occasion" of willing as the pursuit of various values depending on what those values are. However, that apt intuition of Scheler is related not to moral value itself but to the suitability, or rather to the dignity of the person.

Man realizes that dignity through his actions—precisely through the values which he makes an object of pursuit in those actions. In that way, the dignity of the person is somehow re-moved from the sphere of interestedness. In any case, there is here a mutual exclusion in the objective sense: dignity by its essence excludes interestedness.

One can say that the norm of morality requires disinterest-edness in relation to the dignity of the person as an end of action (self-determination). However, one cannot accept that it re-quires indifference in relation to moral value itself as an object of the will. Here—on the contrary—we are witnesses to the most intense pressure: everything that is contained in the reality of an imperative, a categorical one to be precise, acts on the will in such a way that *it definitely wills good* and at the same time *definitely does not will evil*. Here we find ourselves precisely in the area of the deepest *responsibility of man*: the responsibility for my being good or evil as a man—the most fundamental re-sponsibility, the moral responsibility. The character of that re-sponsibility, its subjective and objective measure, constitutes the norm of morality and enters into its determination. It can clearly be seen that the norm of morality can be determined and explained only by investigating its connections with man as the subject of morality.

4. Utilitarianism: Is It Only a Debate About the Foundations of the Norm of Morality?

This issue came to light perhaps most fully and sharply in con-nection with the appearance of Utilitarianism in the history of ethics in the eighteenth century. This was not its first or its only appearance. The issue has its own long history in the development

38

of ethical thought as well as in the human experience of morality. It suffices to mention the various tendencies in ancient Greek thought. However, eighteenth-century Utilitarianism (N.B.: along with the reaction which it evoked in the philosophy of Kant) is to some extent the culmination of that historical debate. In that connection we must also clearly raise the problem of whether this is only a debate about the foundation of the norm and of its establishment in morality, or whether it is even more a debate about very reason for being of ethics, about its "to be or not to be." If, in the realm of contemporary thought, ethics is being subjected to particular questioning, then that is not only the result of positivism, which casts doubt upon the very essence of morality and its objectivization, but also the result of Utilitarianism, which has *fundamentally changed the meaning of moral good and evil,* creating thereby the foundation of the view that moral good and evil as such cannot be apprehended or defined, that we can at most study scientifically that which, in certain conditions, is regarded as or was regarded as morally good or evil.

Historically, the problem of Utilitarianism is connected with the fact to which ancient and medieval ethics (St. Thomas) systematically turned its attention, namely, the fact that, *alongside suitability* (*bonum honestum*), in the field of values proper to man there is also *"utility"* (*bonum utile*) and *"pleasure"* (*bonum delectabile*). In the traditional system, "*utile*" has the character of a means to an end, while "*honestum*" has the character of an end. "*Delectabile,*" on the other hand, has primarily the character of a consequence. Whereas the end is that which a thing pursues (or rather, that on account of which it pursues something), the consequence is that which is achieved in pursuing an end, not necessarily even directly (*per se*), but as though on the side and incidentally (*per accidens*). Such a view of the good, such a threefold axiology, had its full support in the conception of man. On the basis of that conception, morality is strictly connected with suitability, while utility and pleasure draw their moral qualification from suitability. In this way one can also speak about a morality of means (*utile*) and of consequences (*delectabile*), but with the caution that neither the one nor the other can constitute the foundations for the norm or for its establishment in ethics.

Modern Utilitarianism spells the complete demolition of such a view—and that not only in the sphere of axiology, but even more deeply—in the sphere of the conception of man, which perhaps did not appear immediately in its full explication, but only gradually. [N.B.: This suggests that it was precisely Utilitarianism which paved the way for a conception of man that would suit its axiological principles.] In the utilitarian perspective, *man* appears primarily as a *"feeling" subject*, not as a person with his own proper structure of self-possession and self-dominion. In any case, that structure is not fundamental, but secondary. What is fundamental for man is the feeling of pleasure and pain—and that is what primarily sets in motion all the subject's activity. That is, of course, a rational activity, with the qualification that reason serves to "organize" activity only with regard to pleasure or pain. Thence the origin of the primary normative premise of Utilitarianism—*to pursue the maximization of pleasure and the minimization of pain.*

That premise cannot be attacked directly. It is in itself "reasonable" and can also be "suitable." No morality requires the maximization of pain and the minimization of pleasure. Nevertheless, some basic cautions must be raised concerning the foundation of the norm and of its establishment in ethics according to the utilitarian conception. It is easy to see that that system has destroyed the entire sphere of the "suitability," and along with it the "dignity" of man as a person. In connection with that, moral good and evil lost their proper foundation in man and were reduced to their own distinctive kind of pleasure and pain. [Cf. Hume.] *The norm became the computation or calculation* of actions in relation to means and even more in relation to consequences. [N.B.: This calculation is highly problematic, since the consequences are not achieved directly, but only incidentally.]

In connection with Utilitarianism, a theory which has been overcome in the history of ethics [consider the vehement reaction of Kant, and later of phenomenologists], but one whose consequences are still felt—one must ask a basic question: does Utilitarianism signify only a change in the foundation of the ethical norm and its establishment, or is it simply *the annihilation of morality* as such and the negation of ethics? One must come out in favor of the latter: on the principles of utilitarian axiology and anthropology, ethics has no reason for being; it becomes simply unnecessary. On the principles of positivism, ethics is impossible; on the principles of Utilitarianism, it is unnecessary. The fundamental questions of ethics: what exactly ought I to do and why? what is morally good and what is evil, and why?—are, on the principles of positivism, impossible to raise, and on the principles of Utilitarianism—in a sense unnecessary.

5. Utilitarianism and Teleology

We mentioned the triumph of Utilitarianism above, emphasizing at the same time its consequences. I do not intend to go into purely historical considerations here; in this work, I will focus on substantive matters. Nevertheless, it is necessary to say about the *reaction of Kant* both that it had a radical character and that it at the same time proceeded from idealistic and subjectivistic premises. Kant's reaction was a kind of "going to the other extreme." Thus, Kant, recognizing the normative and deontic character of ethics, and of course correctly bringing that very character to light (see Part I), at the same time on the one hand emphasizes the pure apriorism of the norm and of its establishment and on the other takes a position opposed to any kind of teleology in ethics. Had it followed the lines of Kant's principles, ethics would have had a reason for being only as a logic of norms (a deduction of deontic statements). At the same time it would be an ethics in its own way both "static" and abstract, separated from that dynamism which must be proper to ethics because of the activity of the person, activity to which the norms of morality are connected. One must, of course, analyze very precisely the entire mutual relation of ethics and teleology as Kant understands them. There are too many elements here; therefore, it is difficult to present it in its entirety. In any case, in his denial of teleology, Kant accepted, in a certain way, both the utilitarian conception of teleology (and therefore, pleasure and pain as the exclusive ends of human activity and endeavor) and the conception of man which it contains: Man according to Utilitarianism, is before all else the subject of "experience." In the world of "phenomena," and therefore in the range of experience, Kant did not see a different meaning of teleology or the foundations of a different conception of the man–person. That other conception of man he left in the order of the purely "noumenal" and therefore *a priori*. One may say that, in this way, Kant "hid" that which, to a much greater extent than would have resulted from his epistemology, is "revealed." Therefore, phenomenology is the proper reaction to the "radicalism" of Kant.

In particular, it is a matter of the entire *teleological element* in ethics, *at the foundations of the norm and of its establishment.* It is more concretely a matter of whether the norm of morality is—perhaps—in some way connected to teleology or whether such a connection excludes morality, as Kant seems to suggest.

For according to him, no so-called hypothetical norm, no norm of the type: "If you want to achieve *x*, you ought to do *y*," has an ethical character, none designates a moral duty, yet it always contains in itself some kind of Utilitarianism (let us say: interestedness). The ethical norm, in turn, must designate a disinterested duty. With all that, one can and must agree; however, it is difficult to accept that that disinterested duty, "duty for the sake of duty" (*Pflicht aus Pflicht*), has a subjectless or "a-teleological" character. Against that came in turn the reaction of the phenomenologists (Edmund Husserl, Max Scheler, Nicholas Hartmann, Dietrich von Hildebrand).

Referring to the "pre-critical" tradition in ethics, one must accept that duty fully maintains its ethical character if the norm of morality has as its object "goodness as such" (*bonum in se*). From there, morality presupposes in man (the subject and performer of actions) the capacity for cognition, choice, and the realization of precisely that *bonum in se,* the capacity to place it beyond the *bonum utile* as well as beyond the *bonum delectabile.*

And that very capacity, in other words, *the capacity* for cognition, choice, and the *realization of the suitable good (bonum honestum) is the foundation of the ethical norm* and of its establishment. Such a norm and its establishment not only designates the entire field of morality, and defines morality, but at the same time corresponds to the dignity of the man–person as well as serving that dignity. In connection with that, the capacity for choice and for the realization of the *bonum in se* is not found outside the teleology of the man–person. On the contrary, it corresponds to his autorealization and serves the fulfillment of the person. In this sense, morality does not clash with teleology; on the contrary—it as it were grows on its foundation. One other thing, however: how are the end and the norm related to one another? does the end determine the norm, or does the norm rather determine the end? In light of our conclusion so far one must say that *the norm determines the end* (and perhaps within those limits one must accept in ethics the position of Kant); however, that primacy of the norm grows at the same time *on the basis* of teleology, and above all *of the autoteleology of man.*

6. The Norm as the Truth of the Good

Perhaps we have already been sufficiently protected against both Utilitarianism and apriorism in ethics, in the conception of the norm and in its establishment. That which we call "ethical norms" are no interpolation in moral reality. They are an integral part of that reality and are contained in experience as a factor which directly gives rise to moral value. That factor has deep foundations in the structure of self-possession and self-dominion which is proper to the human person. At the same time, this factor transcends the act, each separately considered concretization of the human *agere*. The sense in which it is immanent in relation to the person has already been sufficiently explained.

The immanence of the norm and of its establishment in the human person and in the act of a person is closely connected to the dynamic relation to goodness as such (*bonum honestum*).

Also proper to the person is the capacity to conceptualize that good, and in particular the capacity to conceptualize it when the person becomes the cause of an action—the capacity to conceptualize in act.

In that respect, the conceptualized ethical norm is nothing other than an objectivization (and at the same time a concretization) of the truth of the good, of the good connected with a given action of a person, the good intended in that action and realizable in it. For that reason, the norm is something transcendent in relation to action and to the striving contained in it and directed to some kind of objective value. *The truth of the good takes the form of a concretized judgment,* which to a certain extent remains above the entire dynamism of action–pursuit and which to a certain extent penetrates that action–pursuit as much as possible, wholly influencing its direction. For the judgment itself does not possess the character of a neutral statement: "*x* is good," "*y* is evil," but on that evaluative statement as a foundation rests the entire deontic content: "I ought to do *x*," "I ought not to do *y*." The norm is transcendent in relation to action–pursuit and at the same time is permeated by a dynamism of its own. That deontic dynamism draws its force from the elementary axiology of the being of the person. "I want to be good — I do not want to be evil"—that is not only an ordinary intentional act of will, but is the very reason for being of the person in the axiological order.

That *deontic dynamism,* concretized to particular act, a dynamic of which the foundation and leading element is a judgment about values, is called the voice of conscience. *Conscience,* properly understood, is the constant capacity for rendering such a judgment and for the calculation of the entire deontic dynamism in connection with each act of the person. Conscience is also a fundamental fact of the experience of morality, a fact which tells us to see in normativity an essential and constitutive feature of ethics, and which connects the normativity of ethics with the responsibility of the person, as I try to do here. Also in the conception of ethics the fact of conscience to some extent favors Kant and requires us to subject the traditional metaphysical understanding, dominated as it was by teleology, to a certain correction. At the same time, however, one must say that it is difficult to find any system of philosophy in which the structure of conscience was so thoroughly elaborated as it was in that of St. Thomas. All that has been said so far confirms the Thomistic conception of the relation between synteresis and syneidesis,[1] as well as confirming (although it is expressed somewhat differently) the connection of the act (voice) of conscience with that capacity which St. Thomas calls prudence (*prudentia*). Perhaps in many commentaries the entire idea takes on a too one-sidedly intellectual or rationalistic character—while in reality that "truth of the good," as the norm essentially is, has a fuller character and is not only a truth of thought, but at the same time *a truth of action and a truth of the very being of the person.*

A deontic dynamism based on such a truth is something absolutely new in the world of human pursuits and acts of will and brings into that world—into the world of the "natural" dynamism of the person—the fundamental element of "culture." Duty as a dynamism evoked by the truth of the good at the same time verifies most deeply the entire structure of self-possession and self-dominion and confirms in a most important

3 [Syneidesis is the part of conscience concerned with passing judgment on actions that have already been performed; synteresis, by contrast, serves as a guide with respect to actions not yet undertaken.—Translators]

way the entire reality of the person in man. [Cf. *Person and Act.*] Duty, and through it the truth of the good, in a certain way "slows and holds in place" the whole "natural" dynamism of the subject and at the same time dynamizes it in a completely new way. Conscience always contains a kind of elevation above the "natural" dynamism of the subject, a kind of fixed gaze into the "ideal" world of values—however that gaze is not abstracted from the dynamism of the subject, but rather is assigned to it.

From the point of view of the method proper to the science which ethics is, there is a further possibility which I want only to suggest here (and which I will take up *ex professo* in Part III): that is, namely, *the possibility of some kind of abstraction* of those concrete judgments, in which the truth of the good of human actions is expressed, from that personal-dynamic context in which those judgments in reality fulfill their normative function, and the possibility of considering those judgments somehow in themselves. This abstract way of doing ethics cannot, however, in any way mask the fact that the norm of morality has its fundamental meaning in relation to man and that its proper dimension is that good or evil through which a man as a man becomes, and in reality is, good or evil.

And so also—taking into consideration all the hitherto analyzed aspects of the norm of morality—and especially the final aspect: the truth of the good—we can finally define *the moral norm* as *the rule for being a good man* (as a man) *and acting well.* That rule at the same time demarcates the plane of the reduction of the entire world of norms to the proper "norm of morality." One must at the same time say that the rule for being good and acting well not only applies analogically in the area of a living morality, but of itself shows *analogicality* and not univocity.

Moral value (good — evil) although in itself one, appears

however—with attention to the many-sided character of human action and to the richness and dynamic complexity of the personal subject [see *Person and Act*]—in various forms (e.g., as the values of courage, honesty, love, etc.), of which I will speak later.

7. The Norm and Exemplarism

The analysis of the norm of morality as the immediate foundation of moral value (good—evil) in human action as we have conducted it so far leads us to one more element, one very important for that norm. It is, namely, the element of exemplarism. This is a topic that is very old and fundamental in all branches of philosophy but above all in ethics. It is a topic that continues to arise, especially in contemporary personalistic ethics: in the ethics of values and vocation. A study of the historical development of that topic would have to show us both the difference in the foundations of the old, metaphysical, formulation of exemplary causality (*causa exemplaris*) and of the contemporary phenomenological analysis of the personal exemplar. Regardless of those discrepancies, the fundamental content of exemplarism is common—and it is just that common content that must enter into this study of the norm of morality.

I refer back to the earlier study of deontic dynamism, which is based on the truth of the good. That truth, in the dynamic complex of duties (as the voice of conscience), is always formed on the basis of some kind of *"fixed gaze" at ideal values, which must be realized in the corresponding act*. The norm, and its establishment, always places itself between two "positions" of the same value: between its ideal position and its real one. What is supposed to be realized first is the value *x*, and then in turn it will be realized in the act and in the person. The ethical norm has as its end the realization of the ideal value, i.e., the translation of that which had hitherto manifested itself as something designated to be realized into a state of realization.

That all points to a very fundamental connection of the norm with values and of the establishment of norms with the lived experience of values. That matter has a fundamental significance for the problem of the grounding of ethical norms, which I consider in Part III of this work. A norm, in and of itself, is an expression of a duty, but, as the rule of being good and of acting well, is most fundamentally formulated through values. The fact that those values first occur in the "ideal position" does not in the least address the abstraction from reality. The ideal position of values, in connection with the norm and its establishment, means only that they are an object of thought, are thought of, before they become a property of a real subject—it does not, however, mean that the values are "thought up." They are thought of as elements of the fulfillment of the subject "man" in the act of the person. For they point to that subject as a reality in development, in actualization, in the process of perfection. They determine the realistic directions of that process and of that actualization. Those "realistic" directions are not "idealistic" before their realization, although they are in the "ideal" position.

Thus the property of the ethical norm, its essential profile, is a very specific knowledge about man in general, about concrete man: *what he is supposed to be.* That image enters into that truth of the good which the norm expresses—and in its own way ensures that it is not some "neutral" truth but truth as the content of duty. Through that truth, duty somehow imitates that "ideal" image and in accordance with it directs man's action: leads to the realization of the ideal. *The ideal, imitation,* and *exemplarism* indirectly touch on various acts, actions of the person, while they directly and fundamentally touch the person himself. Thus one must judge on the basis of the content of various norms, normative statements, commands and prohibitions. They all immediately and directly speak about some kind of content of action (e.g., thou shalt not steal, honor thy father and mother). However, that content remains connected to the realization of a certain "ideal," the one identifying what a man in general ought to be and what an individual man ought to be. [We always situate ourselves in light of those two kinds of questions: what ought I to do? and what is good and what is evil?] One may even say: I ought to do *x* or *y* because *x* or *y* correspond to the ideal—to the image of a good man, from which arises the need for the reflection of *x* or *y* in a concrete act.

If it is a matter of the difference between command and prohibition: "I ought to do"—"I ought not to do," then precisely that second kind of norm and its establishment seems to be particularly remote from the transfer of the ideal and the reproduction of the ideal value into act. However, on closer analysis we must come to realize that prohibitions do contain just such a foundation. Here also it is a matter of realizing the ideal value of man—although the *negative form of expression*, the negative formulation of a normative statement, *indicates* only *a higher degree of threat to that ideal*, a greater contradiction with the image of man: what he ought to be. Therefore, the negative form of a normative statement (a prohibition) somehow signifies a greater deontic dynamization than does the positive form. Connected with this is the whole problem of the greater distinctness of moral evil, guilt, and sin in experience and in literature.

The element of exemplarism is to some extent the most

deeply hidden internal contentful element of the norm, and at the same time seems to be the element that is most external and most evident in the existential, interpersonal and social order. The establishment of norms is realized, to a significant extent *by way of imitating* personal exemplars. The entire process of exemplification mentioned above, the transfer of values from ideal to real states, has its real foundation in that order and system. It is for that reason that Aristotle gives primary attention to "the good man;" it is for that reason that the Gospel so often speaks of "imitation [or 'following'—Transl.]," and for that reason that all of contemporary ethics—after the period of Kantian apriorism in the interpretation of duty—is returning with such determination to those same means—example and imitation. Man is an example for man, an example that attracts or one that repels. The element of exemplarism inscribes itself into the ethical norm directly and through experience, intuitively, thereby indicating at the same time how fundamental are the categories of good and evil in thinking, acting, and in the lives of people.

8. Ethics—A Normative Science or a Practical One?

Such an immediate, intuitive character is ascribed to the statement: *"bonum est faciendum, malum vitandum"*—"good is to be done, and evil avoided," in which traditional ethics saw the first principle of all practical thought and—through the connection of morality with the practical order—at the same time saw the first principle of ethics, the philosophy of morality: synteresis, practical judgment, from which all further judgments, ever more particular, draw their force. They draw those conclusions via the syllogism, which allows us, from the above-named principle as a major premise, to draw conclusions after stating in the minor premise what is good and what is evil: *x* is good, therefore *faciendum, y* is evil, therefore *vitandum*.

There is no way to oppose the soundness of this view. One must also notice that the *primum principium practicum* [first practical principle] refers not only to ethics but also to technics—and in the field of workmanship one must take direction from that same general principle: the workman also ought to do his work well and not to do it badly. One can extend the principle further to all so-called norms of adaptation or even to legal norms.

However, the essential problem which must be treated here is different. It is first of all a matter of the *proper nature of the primum principium: bonum est faciendum, malum vitandum*—and second *whether it is really the central principle of ethics*. In traditional ethics [cf. St. Thomas] the matter is put just that way.

Such a formulation of the problem was connected with the entire conception of cognition and of philosophy. Ethics was, in this conception, the domain of practical cognition and the main field of practical philosophy. The principle of synteresis was at the center of that cognition and of that philosophy as the principle which connects practice with theory, returning the acting subject to the previously known truth in which he had always found a ready answer to the question: what is good and what is evil? That theory was simultaneously ontological and axiological. Ethics was an extension of metaphysics, emerging from it on the basis of the key principle of synteresis, whose *immediate evidence* left no room for doubt. In such a position, it was essentially that field of philosophy in which we answer the question: what must one do?—i.e., practical philosophy.

It seems, however, that in modern philosophy a fuller

understanding of ethics has been achieved. That fuller understanding contains two elements:

1. A fuller and broader account of the moral fact

2. In connection with that, the posing of new questions which, in relation to the older questions—what must one do, and what must one avoid?—are deeper and more enriching.

These are questions that have been already been cited many times: what is morally good and what is morally evil and why? One must note that *these questions somehow move the central problematic of ethics* one entire step *back*. The questions are aimed at the central reality of the norm of morality and make it the main topic of investigation, while the earlier questions— what must one do, and what must one avoid?—rather simply presupposed the reality of the norm of morality. It also seems that on that orientation is based a fundamental transformation as a result of which *ethics becomes above all a normative science, and only indirectly a practical one*—while according to the traditional conception it was a science that was first of all practical.

The principle of synteresis—*bonum faciendum, malum vitandum*—is in itself not so much the very principle of being good and of acting well and in that sense the norm of morality: an answer to the question: what is good and what is evil?—as it is a principle of practice, a *principle of the translation of norms into the order of action* and of realization, in which sense it is also a principle of the practice of morality.

It is not difficult to notice that that whole *turn in ethics*, following the line of those new questions which (as was already mentioned) seem to correspond better to morality as a fact given in experience, in a particular way *expands the traditional minor*

premise of the practical syllogism, and in a particular way emphasizes it. That does not mean a disengagement from the practical
order, it means only a more penetrating entry into that which,
in the practical order, determines morality. The principle *bonum
faciendum, malum vitandum* as the first premise of every practical syllogism, does not give rise to any doubts. Meanwhile the
essential problem of ethics is found in the minor premise, in
the statement: *x est bonum; y est malum* [*x* is good; *y* is bad].
On it depends the proper ethical meaning of the entire practical
syllogism—and therefore on it must be focused the entire cognitive effort in the philosophy of morality. The answer to the
question: what is morally good and what is evil—and why?, pre-
determines the ethical meaning of the entire practical realm,
and not the other way around.

In that sense one may, and even must, speak about *some
kind of revolution* which has occurred in the ethics of modern
times. The substantive subordination of practicality to normativity had to bring with it, not so much (as in the case of Kant)
the rejection of the entire teleological structure which had hitherto been dominant, but its demotion. The earlier dominance
of teleology is fully understandable given the basic principle that
ethics is primarily a practical philosophy and that praxis-action
unfolds in relation to an end. It seems, therefore, that as, a side
effect of that substantive change in the conception of ethics as
"not a practical science, but a normative one," there developed
a so-called praxiology.

At the same time, however, one must say that that whole
substantive turn towards normativity has an indirect significance for the very practicality of ethics. Still it is matter precisely
of action, about the doing of good and the avoidance of evil—

but in such a way that both the doing and the avoidance are accomplished as comprehensively as possible. It is a matter of *a thorough knowledge of the nature of moral good and evil* in human actions. And that direction of development in ethics seems fully to correspond to the development of human consciousness.

PART III

The Natural Law and the Personalistic Norm

1. The Full Profile of Ethics

THE CONCEPTION OF ETHICS DEVELOPED IN THIS STUDY RE-mains closely connected to experience. At the center of attention is always the concrete man along with the field of responsibility proper to him, one which has the character of moral responsibility. In Part II I tried to show that just such a character of responsibility supports a normative conception of ethics; at the same time the considerations raised in that part of the book were concentrated on the essence of the norm of morality (what is a norm?). That problem can be resolved *in a theoretical way only to a certain extent*—and only to a certain extent belongs to the theory of morality. To the extent, namely, that the analysis of every fact given in the experience of morality reveals in its deontic dynamism a relation to an indicator of duty, to the principle of being good and acting well.

However, the problem of the norm does not allow itself either to be posed or fully to be fully resolved within the limits of a theory of morality. It is impossible to answer the question: what is the moral norm?, without answering the question: *what is a norm?* That question is most often met with the preliminary questions of ethics dictated by the experience of morality. Those questions are, as we know: what in fact ought I to do—and why?, and corresponding to it, at a more general level: what is morally good and what evil—and why? Contained in those questions, of course, is a question about the norm of morality, but it is not so much, what it is as what kind of thing it is.

As can be seen, ethics presupposes a particular "limit" of theory, and so of a concrete theory of morality. Ethics incorporates itself into the theory, but is not itself that theory. It introduces its profile throughout the theory, a profile which—as was once thought—is the profile of a practical science and of practical cognition, or, as is currently thought, is rather the profile of a normative science. There is also the matter of a more precise specification of *what is meant by a "normative science."* For "science" [*nauka*][1] could mean: the science of the norm (norms) of morality, but it could also mean: the teaching of the norms of morality (moralizing *sui generis*). It seems that neither the first of these conceptions (which, it should be noted, is close to the principles of positivism) nor the second (which is close to the principles of apriorism) completely answer the preliminary questions of ethics and as a result do not continue the traditional "perennial" style of that science.

For above all, ethics was from the beginning *a field of philosophy*, philosophical knowledge, for which—according to the classical thought of the Stagirite—what is proper is the

---

1 [The Polish word *nauka* can mean either *science* or *teaching* (or even *doctrine*).—Translators]

formulation of all problems, of all of reality, *in light of ultimate causes*. It is known that the development of the particular sciences over the centuries, especially in the modern period, tore many branches away from an initially unified "philosophy" and made for them a domain of their own. In connection with that there arose the following question: whether ethics cannot itself be separated from the field of philosophy and conducted in a way similar to the other particular sciences. The revolution in the traditional understanding of ethics which has been carried out—and accepted here to a certain extent—shows, however, with all its consequences, that that science, even in its new formulation, "manifests" its need for ultimate causes, for resolution *per ultimas causas*. Perhaps that need is even clearer today, in the face of a decidedly empirical point of departure and in the face of the promotion of the normative character of ethics above the practical.

That need remains in the preliminary questions themselves, which accompany the experience of morality both in the more individual version and in the general version. For in the context of the unarguable fact of moral duty, we ask: what ought I to do—and why? We ask also: what is morally good and what is evil—and why? Through that "why" we demand not only an indication of the ethical norm, but also its *justification*. And in that sense we displace the entire problematic to ultimate causes, *ad ultimas causas*. In that way the true philosophical dimension of ethics is revealed; it is revealed anew, after all the transformations to which its conception was subjected and after all the attempts to "lead" the problems of ethics away from the dimension of philosophy in order to place it within the dimension of the particular sciences.

That philosophical dimension of ethics is revealed,

however, *in a way other* than it was in the tradition conception, and on different principles. It is perhaps revealed in a more homogenous way. In order to shed light on that, one must return again to the contemporary debates about the logical value of normative statements. Logicians are inclined to deny them logical status, placing them outside the boundaries of truth and falsity—thereby excluding them from the terrain of science. Along with normative statements, ethics itself loses its civic rights on that terrain insofar as it is considered to be (and often is) a set of imperative statements. N.B.: One can see in that a particular crisis of the ethics of the "pure imperative," an ethics understood as teaching morality via the simple deduction of norms. It is appropriate in this context to say that if the view about the non-scientific character of ethics (as a set of imperative statements) which the logicians have disseminated seems to cut the roots of that science, they are not the ones from which it really grows.

We have seen many times that ethics does not grow as a simplistic collection of imperative statements, but as an organic response to man's eternal question about good and evil. I will try to explain later the extent to which that collection of imperative statements enters the structure of ethics. For now, it is certain that *ethics*, together with people from all ages, *is searching for the answer to the question: what is morally good and what is evil—and why?* And that search, as can be seen from the very character of the question, has a *philosophical* dimension and tends to show the proper nature [*ratio*] of all our moral duties, including the ultimate ones.

Asking about moral good and evil, we are asking in a specific sense about truth and falsity. In the area of human decisions (and so in the area of practice), that true–false has primarily the meaning of "right–wrong." However, the norms of morality can also be formulated and discussed outside the area of decisions, outside of practice, to a certain extent in themselves. It is exactly then above all that the "truth of the good," which is the primary content of each of those norms, manifests itself. That "*truth of the good*" is in some way a *superordinate category in relation to "right"* (and "wrong"). A given decision is right because it contains precisely the truth of the good and it is wrong if it does not correspond to it. The truth of the good is an essential element of each ethical norm; however, the form which that truth takes in the "deontic connection"—the form of the imperative statement—is already something secondary and accidental.

It is just in connection with the fact that each ethical norm contains essentially some kind of truth of the good (which was already discussed in Part II), that the primary question of ethics, which asks: what is morally good and what is evil—and why?, makes sense. If we ask about the proper and ultimate nature [*ratio*] of moral good and evil, it means that we see the foundation of the answer to such a question and we acknowledge its sense.

The philosophical dimension of ethics (according to the profile sketched here) is connected to the conviction that *each norm of morality* has primarily the character of *a theoretical judgment*, and only secondarily an imperative form. The first operation (and a relatively easy one) is to extract from that form the judgment about good and evil, which it includes. It contains precisely *implicite* the judgment about good and evil, and not only about good itself or evil itself, considering the opposite character of ethical values. Of course there is still the possibility of considering goodness itself or evil itself. But what is that about? It is precisely about the justification of a norm—i.e., indication of the proper causes [*ratio*], possibly the ultimate ones, which explain "why *x* is good and *y* is evil." It is, therefore, a kind of "reduction."

That reduction is based on the clarification of proper axiological relations on ontological foundations. [It is presupposed by the conviction that axiology has precisely such foundations—that is another topic, and a broad one.]

In the categories of the philosophy of language one could speak about *the reduction of norms to evaluations*, presupposing the difference between evaluation and description.

Finally, it seems that the profile of ethics so understood (as a "philosophical" profile) situated itself, to a certain extent, in the traditional profile of a practical science (which was also philosophical), namely—the traditional conception of ethics, which comes from synteresis as from a *primum principium practicum*, presupposed that the entire "justification of norms," the answer to the question: what is good and what is evil—and why? is already contained in the theoretical part of philosophy. In ethics one must only ask the question: what must be done, and what must be avoided in light of the previously constructed theory. We said above that the revolution carried out on the terrain of the conception of ethics in the modern period is based on the particular development of the minor premise of the practical syllogism. When, however, someone thinks that such a formulation explains the problem fully, he may be wrong.

2. The Limits of a Practical Science

In offering an account of a conception of ethics as a practical science we do not deny its practicality. We are only trying to lay for that practicality a sound foundation. That is shown by the way we have analyzed the problem so far. It is hard to deny that in ethics practicality is based on normativity. When we have to answer the question: what must one do?, and to do so on the basis of the principle, *bonum faciendum, malum vitandum*, we must determine as honestly as possible *quid sit bonum et malum?*: what is morally good, and what is evil and why?—i.e., to answer the question to which we have constantly been returning as to the main question of ethics in its normative conception.

For that reason, we have agreed that the first principle of the practical order, synteresis, is more than anything the principle of transferring an answer already prepared for the question about moral good and evil over to the practical order. That principle essentially leads us into the realm of praxis, leads us most directly and most obviously—but with the support of a normative base: it leads us on the basis of an already accepted and internally approved truth of the moral good (or of evil). That element of the internal acceptance and approbation of the truth of the moral good (or of evil) we call conscience—the judgment of conscience. That judgment possesses a character which might be described as the "lowermost" (in differentiation from the "uppermost," which would be the reason [*ratio*] which ultimately justifies the norm). St. Thomas sees in the judgment of conscience: *iudicium ultimo-practicum*, the ultimate element in the transfer of the principle of being good and acting well into the order of action, the ultimate element in the embodiment of the principle into act. It is another thing, however, that this judgment of conscience is also *iudicium practico-practicum*, i.e., purely practical: "fulfill *x*," "do not do *y*." The structure of conscience manifests rather complexity, into which enter not only practical elements, but also theoretical ones: "fulfill *x*, because it is good," "do not do *y*, because it is evil." And thus, one gets a command (or a prohibition) resulting from evaluation—and that in relation to a given act, the final evaluation.

Now we must take up the matter of *what role science can play* in relation to the process of the "transfer" to the practical order as sketched above. In other words: what are the possibilities of a practical science (of ethics as a practical science)? It is clear, that it can help to make a norm more precise, i.e., the principle of being good and acting well with respect to a concrete act which one must perform. That direction has the name of *casuistry* (it is so called not only in the field of morality but above all in that field). One can formulate the rule about performing a given act ever more precisely, taking into consideration various—possibly all—the circumstances, both objective and subjective, that surround it. Casuistry is, however, always an attempt to formulate in theory what "is itself" in practice. In that way, however, the ever more precise "alignment" of the norm to concrete human actions remains always beyond the concrete, beyond the concrete existential decision. It is an attempt to approximate the concrete, somehow "from without."

The final concretization of the norm *iudicium ultimo-practicum* is somehow always realized "from within;" it is an act of conscience. And only in that dimension does it possess its own practicality. We can also clearly approximate that sphere externally, somehow from outside the subject. Perhaps the so-called *directing of conscience* is more important here than is the more abstract casuistry. *The practical sciences*, apparently, *have limits which cannot be crossed.* Those limits result, firstly, from the general impossibility of the complete objectification of that which is subjective; secondly, from the complete originality of every act of will, of every decision and act of self-determination.

That does not, by any means, however, show that ethics makes no sense as a practical science. The entire process of the alignment of norms with human actions, conducted in a scientific way, is very useful for the morality of those actions—however, under the sole condition that we are aware of the limits of ethics as a practical science. That awareness and that conviction do not, however, by any means, lead to the acceptance of the view which is sometimes called situation ethics.

Situation ethics accepts as a primary principle (which it takes from existentialism), the conviction that any objectivization of that which is subjective is impossible. Against that background, the possibility of the ethical norm is excluded in the sense that a completely and purely subjective decision cannot be brought into conformity with any objective truth about the good (even if such were otherwise possible). On those principles the full originality of human self-determination and decision-making would be based on the fact that it is *only the answer to the given "situation"*: to the situation in the internal and the external sense. In that answer, the subject himself would "create" good or evil beyond any norms of morality. Situation ethics is also a kind of *new form of autonomism*—however, one much more advanced in its denial of essential elements of ethics and of anthropology and indirectly of the experience of the human being and of morality.

It would be difficult to give a complete account of that subject here. It is appropriate, however, to state that the boundary of ethics as a practical science to which we made reference, must be situated between an exaggerated casuistry and a situation ethics. It is a line of demarcation separating the substance of ethics itself from both of those deviations.

3. The Limits of a Normative Science

If we place the norm, i.e., a principle of being good as a man and of acting well (or not being evil and not acting badly), at the center of ethics, the question arises of how we can get scientifically to the construction, and above all to the formulation, of that principle. Asking that question, we will find ourselves—as in Part I, only on a higher level—at the very center of the debate between empiricism and apriorism. That debate permeates the whole history of ethics and constantly places us somehow at the brink of its annihilation.

It is appropriate to remark here that *ethics as a science does not have as its end the creation of the norms of morality.* One may say that it is like grammar, which also does not have as its end the creation of the rules of a language. Grammar reads these rules from actual human speech, observes the facts from there, and proceeds to establish the regularities which are present in the language itself, being somehow present "by nature." And in that way grammar also takes on the marks of a normative science: it brings to light the rules which govern a language—actual speech—and in turn requires alignment to them.

It seems that the task of ethics is similar. Similarly also must be conceived its meaning as a normative science. It is, at the same time, also somehow a further stage and a "higher level" in the understanding and interpretation of the morality given in experience, which we discussed in Part I. In that morality, of course, there are various kinds of norms, as we already said in Part II. To ethics belongs not so much an inductively conducted identification of those norms, or even their elimination (selection) leaving only those which are the real norms of morality. Inductive methods in the positivist sense, like the method of deduction, have here perhaps a secondary and auxiliary meaning. Fundamental is *the method of particular reduction*, through which we determine—primarily intuitively—how much the principle of being good as a man and acting well (or not being evil and not acting badly) is realized in a given prescription of behavior (commands, prohibitions, etc.).

One must note that in that case that cognitive process concerns not the concrete act, as is the case in casuistry, but concerns the very norms, the very principles of human conduct. Ethics as a normative science does not entitle us to establish these norms, but it requires their recognition in a systematic way and then their justification, as was discussed before.

How is such a recognition of the norms of morality to be conducted? On what is it based? It is based on the conviction that one or another principle of behavior really contributes to the formation of moral values and that behavior in accordance with them makes a man good, while behavior contrary to it makes him evil as a man. That conviction is shared by all, including the ethicist and the moralist. The latter read them somehow in human life, both personal and social, and later make them more precise using the appropriate methods of science.

It is known that the principles of behavior are recorded not only in the lives and convictions of people, but also formally recorded in written sources. They are the *written codices of morality* which come to the assistance of the convictions of men and nations. If we find in those codices some divergences and differentiation in details and in secondary matters, then at the same time we find convergence and unity in primary matters and in the general lines of the guiding principles of morality. There are many written codices, from different times, differing in quality and in range of interest. Of one quality are, for example, the Gospels and the holy books containing the *moralia* of different religions; of another, the *ad hoc* published codes of morality (e.g., guides for tourists, etiquette books, etc.). However, alongside the formal record one must take into consideration that second—though really first—*record, the one found in human convictions*. In it, the fate of the various legal codes of morality is determined, the meaning of norms contained in those codices is preserved or lost, and the hierarchy of those norms is maintained—the conviction about the superiority of certain norms or even certain systems in relation to others, etc.

A positivist might say here: all that shows that a science about morality can concern itself only and exclusively about what people—in various social circles or in various conditions—considered or consider as good or evil. The aspiration of a normative science can go no further. *Ethics*, however, *must raise a question that does go further*: what is morally good and what is evil?—and sees the possibility of giving an answer supported by an experiential foundation. The method of getting that answer is *the reduction* of all norms to those fundamental ones about which we can say with complete certainty that they are principles of "being good as a man and acting well." In that reduction, as can be seen, anthropology, the axiology of man, and above all the concept of his dignity (*honestum*) must have fundamental significance.

Looking from that perspective at the complete set of norms recorded in the codices of morality and in the lives of man and of society, we are able to ascertain that *some of them* are principles of being good and acting well *which are immediately evident* (e.g., thou shalt not kill, thou shalt not steal, thou shalt not commit adultery, etc.); *others* become evident *only via some kind of reasoning process* or clarification. According to St. Thomas,

sometimes a short and easy process of reasoning will be sufficient, and sometimes a longer argument will be necessary in
order to "derive" a particular norm from the immediately evident, or at least more evident, principle. That process of the
"*derivation*" of norms, along with the process of "verification,"
comes to permeate ethical reflection. It is not, in this case, a
matter of verification, of whether people are applying one or
another principle of behavior in their lives, but it is a matter of
the verification of the very principle in all its normative varia-
tions, in various applications depending on conditions, etc.

If all of that makes up the remote and diversified reality
which we call "morality"—then one must admit that aside from
synteresis (the principle *bonum faciendum, malum vitandum*),
man understood in the broadest and most general sense is
equipped with another principle, *superior in relation to the first*,
one whose content is not primarily practical but primarily normative: *hoc est bonum, istud malum* [this is good; that is evil].
Within those limits of such a generally formulated principle,
there is *a possibility of fulfilling with a concrete*—and of course,
ever more precise—*content* that *hoc quod est bonum*, as well as
that *istud quod est malum*. What is more, there are here certain
contents, more or less obvious, and the possibility reaching
greater evidence in relation to the normative contents which are
at first less evident.

It seems that precisely that *structure of the normative foundations,* which is in some way the common property of all "normal" people, is contained in the concept of a "natural law." It is
the first meaning of the concept, but not the only one, as we
will see later. Speaking about "normal" people, I have in mind
people with average personal and social development. In particular, I can refer that normality to the so-called moral sense

(moral sensitivity, sound conscience) whose opposite is so-called "moral insanity."

Therefore, as follows from what was said above, the moral foundation in man shows a dynamic of its own. The principles of behavior have their own direct obviousness, or they can become obvious indirectly. All the processes of the derivation or even of the verification of norms are at work here. That shows that the natural law, in the first sense which I am giving the term, is not some kind of rigid and closed system. It is a "flexible" system of its own. The flexibility of that system is entirely based on values as a content, on the one hand objective and transcendent—and on the other hand, subjectively knowable and experienced.[2] The whole problem of the *justification of norms* (discussed in this part) *is based on the discovery of these axiological relations and the corresponding ontic foundations.* Those foundations allow one to make particular principles of behavior obvious, and allow one to ascertain that the principle contains the foundational principle of being good as a man and acting well—and that it contains it to a greater or lesser extent. For moral values also show their own form of gradation or even of "hierarchy." It is sufficient to ascertain that, in addition to mediocrity, there is heroism; in addition to moral correctness, there is exemplary virtue, etc.

For it seems that through all that people recognized or recognize as morally good or evil, it is possible—possible and indispensable—to know what is a good and what an evil. Even more: one can say that only for that reason have people recognized and do they recognize x as good, y as evil, *because there is in general*

2   Wojtyła's word here refers precisely to what we have called "lived experience."—Translators.

moral goodness and evil. People are above all aware of that fact, and that awareness, like an empty field, comes to be filled with its own content.

4. The Natural Law

By "natural law" I mean not only that fundamental structure of the normative foundation which I tried to sketch above. I mean by it also a certain *method of justification of the norms of human morality.* It is appropriate to discuss that method now. However, before doing that, it is necessary to realize that by "natural law" is most often meant that very set of the norms of human morality which are not only the most fundamental, but are at the same time "unwritten." They do not make up any historical codification of the principles of morality, but they do serve simultaneously as the foundation for all codification, make it possible, and verify it. That "unwritten codex" is simultaneously most deeply and most essentially recorded in the moral consciousness of man. It is well-known that there has been a fierce debate about "natural law" in that sense with the representatives of positivist thought. Objection to natural law comes also from antitheistic premises and attitudes because—not without reason—it is seen as including a trace of interference from above—Divine interference—in human morality. The natural law is the "codex" of the Creator himself, inscribed into the very being of man and of the world—and kept accessible to man as a rational being: knowable for and realizable by him.

One must also grasp correctly *the transcendental character* of that law along with its simultaneous *immanence* in man and in the world. Immanence is embodied in the fact that the natural law is inscribed in the very being of man and of the world, in the fact that the natural law is in some way identical with that very being. On what is its transcendence based? It will be necessary to formulate and to clarify it in several steps or aspects. The transcendent element proper to the natural law is already certainly the element of the objective truth of the good of all being, an element which outgrows any subjective lived experience of values or even of any subjective striving for values. We will return to the problem of the "immanence—transcendence" of the natural law later.

First it is necessary to concentrate on the concept of a "natural law" to the extent that it both designates and determines a certain method of justifying the norms of morality, i.e., to the extent that it leads us to fulfillment of the definitive tasks of ethics. For we notice those tasks (*cognitio per ultimas causas* [knowledge through ultimate causes]) precisely in the justification of norms. The justification of the norms of morality depends on the discovery of the axiological system which supports that, but not any other, concept or even formulation of the norm, and for that, but not any other, concretization of the principle of being good as a man and acting well (or, not being evil and not acting badly). That axiological system is always somehow rooted in ontic structures. Natural law points to the need for penetration into that ontic structure and to the need *to understand natures, i.e. the essences of things*, essences which enter into the object of a human action. The basis of the justification of norms is precisely and primarily that understanding of natures, a penetration into the entire essential order of the reality of man and of the world. *In that order are rooted* all the systems and *axiological relations* which themselves make a separate order, but one connected with the ontic order.

The natural law assumes that being and values are in some way connected to one another and mutually dependent. The natural law also assumes that beings (natures) and values are organized into a certain order which is, directly or at least indirectly, accessible to human cognition and which attains in that cognition its obviousness. Certain phenomenologists (e.g., Scheler), who take values to be irreducible to being, seem to oppose that conviction, asserting at the same time that values are accessible to a certain kind of feeling (*Wertfühlen*), although they escape rational cognition. It seems, however, that the traditional conception, which admits its own kind of reducibility of the good (values) to being, and consequently some kind of overlap and mutual dependence of the axiological and the ontological order, still remains the correct conception and it must be maintained.

[In this place should perhaps go some kind of very broad argument on the mutual relation of ontology and axiology and on the cognition of being and values.]

Accepting the natural law as such a method for justifying the norms of morality, one must at the same time emphasize strongly that to that method must belong not only the very understanding of natures (of the essences of things) but also the formulation of axiological relations and their interconnections. Both one and the other are functions of a particular kind of intuition (*intus-legere*) of reality which is the object (*objectum circa quod*) of human actions. In each action there is some reference to that reality. That reference is correct to the extent that there is realized in it a proper understanding of both orders: of being and of values. And it is just that that is contained in the concept of "natural law."

5. The Personalistic Norm

I introduce the concept of the "personalistic norm" here also from the point of view of method: just as does "natural law," it signifies a certain *method of justification for the norms of morality.* This method is not opposed to the natural law, but *complementary* to it and its place in ethics results from the fact that, as a matter of fact, the set of norms appearing in human morality primarily defines the principle *of reference to the person*: the principle of reference to one's own person (to be good as a man) and also—at least indirectly—some kind of principle of reference to another (second) person or persons. However, in order better to explain the meaning of the personalistic norm as a method of justification for the particular norms of morality, let us look at it at first in a comparative way, perhaps even to some extent historically.

The natural law as a norm or as a set of the norms of morality indicates above all the fact that *man*—the author of acts and the author of moral values—*remains in the world, in the multiplicity of beings and of natures,* as one of them. Human action is laden with duties towards the world, ought to serve its affirmation and construction, and must not lead to its destruction or devaluation. In relation to normative truth accentuated in that way, the personalistic norm tries to emphasize the *particular position of man as a person* and the distinctness and transcendence which result from it. That does not mean separation from the order of nature and even less its cancellation—quite the contrary, the personalistic norm signifies a deeper penetration into the world of natures in order, on the normative plane, to extract more fully the "nature of man" who, by his very nature, is a person. And therefore, on the basis of natural law, what is required is the formulation of a principle or principles which fully correspond to that reality.

Among the historical codices of morality, it is the Gospel above all that contains such a formulation (from which flows all that is distinctive in Christian morality).

In the history of philosophy and of ethics, it was Immanuel Kant who made a particular contribution to the formulation of the personalistic norm with his analysis of the categorical imperative. Kant's so-called second formulation postulates that a person should always be only the end of an action and never exclusively a means to an end. In that formulation, Kant had in mind the postulate of Utilitarianism (see above), which he correctly appraised—and with respect to which he saw the need to protect the person as well as the axiological position (dignity) of the person in action.

Making the transition from those elements of a living morality and of the history of ethics to the heart of our problem, one must say that the personalistic norm is the primary principle of human acts, according to which all the actions of man in any field whatsoever must be *adjusted* to the *relation "to the person"* which is fundamental in human action. That relation is truly contained in every human action regardless of how much that action, in its objective content, could seem to be "matter-of-fact." All moral sensibility is based on uncovering, in our acts, the personal element as a "purely human" element which, through all the "purely matter-of-fact" fabric of the content of our action, continually manages to show through. Man's action is not, in the final analysis, primarily the realization of the world, but *the realization of himself: of humanity and of the person.* Besides that, human action is realized despite all "matter-of-fact" structures (or "matter-of-fact" barriers) primarily in interpersonal relations: for the person enters from the objective side into the norm of action as a fundamental reality and value to which the norm of morality must, in the first place, adjust.

Every man contributes, in his actions, in the first place, to the realization of the world of persons in a positive or negative direction. The fact that human action is sometimes to a great extent co-operation (action together with others) contributes even more to the emphasis on the personalistic norm. [Cf. *Person and Act*.]

Finally, the previously discussed complementarity of two elements—the immanent and transcendent elements of morality—support this. If the normative order is to some extent completely written into the order of being and of nature—then still it becomes natural law through being deciphered by man, by being somehow *elevated* to the level of mind and spirit, *to the level of the person*. In that way, also that order ceases to be given only as a "world of necessity," becoming instead assigned to man in his proper world of freedom. It becomes a genuine participation in Eternal Law, *participatio legis aeternae in rationali creatura* [participation of the eternal law in the rational creature].

Moving from those thoughts to the one expressed at the beginning: the personalistic norm indicates a direction for the justification of the norms of human morality. It is a direction—as follows from the earlier considerations—somewhat different from the direction of the natural law, although it is rather complementary than opposed to it. [*Love and Responsibility* can serve as an example here.] Understanding justification thus, we can take into consideration in a particular way those axiological relations which are proper to the person and flow out of his ontic reality. For we take into consideration the truth about the transutilitarian significance of the person, about his auto-teleology, which excludes taking him as a "means to an end"—finally, we take into consideration the particular value of love which, as a principle of behavior, best corresponds to that reality which a person is.

6. The Unity of the Norm and the Multiplicity of Norms

The problem of "the unity of the norm and the multiplicity of norms" is in some way presupposed in all the conclusions we have reached thus far. It is contained in the concept of natural law as well as in the concept of the personalistic norm and finally, from a different perspective—in the entire concept of the deduction of norms and of their "verification." The world of norms is *not only multi-faceted, but also multi-layered.* It contains norms which are, in relation to other norms, "superior" and "inferior" or "secondary." Some depend on others and some are explained by others. The world of norms can appear to us as an area of deduction—if we assume that the superior, or fundamental, norm is known to us and obvious for us, then we can also, proceeding from it by way of reasoning, arrive at subordinate norms. It seems, however, that that world of norms *is rather the area of reduction,* an area on which we try to get to the obviousness of particular principles of behavior, reducing them to the simple and obvious principle of "being good as a man and of acting well." The justification of norms—considered in this part of the book—is implicated in this reductive process. For the clarification of the corresponding axiological relations on ontic foundations helps us to understand that, in a given norm, the fundamental principle of being good and of acting well is truly realized. In that way, the tasks of ethics enter into the warp of lived, existential morality.

When, however, I speak about the unity of the norm and the multiplicity of norms, I have in mind still another system of ethics that has been elaborated on the basis of experience. I am talking about a system which, in the ethical tradition, is sometimes considered in the context of aretology as a system of *moral virtues (or vices)*. That system depends on the correctly perceived fact that the moral value good–evil appears in many different forms, which are qualitatively different from one another. In that way, the experience of morality allows us to extract as forms of good–evil, e.g., justice–injustice, temperance–intemperance, courage–cowardice, etc. In that broad and differentiated field of moral values, traditional ethics achieved not only their identification, but also their correct systematization, the result of which is, e.g., the Thomistic doctrine of cardinal virtues, of the relation of all other virtues to them (*partes virtutum*) and of the relation of the virtues to one another (*nexus virtutum*).

In that traditional doctrine the problem of the unity of the norm and the multiplicity of norms is contained in a capital way. Since norms are those principles of action, of human acts, to which the various forms of moral good and evil (on the basis of their agreement or their disagreement with norms) directly owe their appearance in those acts—then the simple, elementary, and general principle of being good and of acting well "splinters" (as can be seen from experience and according to traditional ethics) into many more particular normative principles, namely *the principles of the virtues (or vices)*. The translation of those principles into practice is ultimately based on synteresis, and their realization in practice gives us acts which qualitatively differ among themselves just as do the very principles of action which serve as their foundation. In that way, aretology enters the realm of the ethical norm.   It is rather a consequence of the traditional doctrine in this area. For traditionally, aretology signifies axiological multiplicity in ethics (the multiplicity of varieties and forms of moral good–evil). Even more, in ethics it signifies the multiplicity of moral capacity—from that point of view the issues connected to the virtues and vices become a part of pedagogy (so-called educational ethics). In that formulation, however—which seems to be essentially an ethical formulation—we see above all a multiplicity of norms, a multiplicity systematized on the basis of the experience of morality and the traditions of ethics and norms which meet in the fundamental unity of the ethical norm. That multiplicity allows us not only to conduct the science of ethics in a particular way, but steadily to deepen it.

Index